101 Tips to Win Your Social Security Disability Claim

Avi Leibovic, Esq.

Dedication

This book is dedicated to my loving wife, Rena, who has been a constant source of blessings and support.

I don't know what I would do without you in my life!

You are my everything.

I Love You.

Avi

Note of Appreciation

IS ANY BOOK COMPLETE without giving a sincere Note of Appreciation to one's mother?

Of course not!

If not for my mother, who pushed me to go to law school, I am pretty confident that you wouldn't be holding this book in your hand, and I would not have been able to help the millions of people who have watched my videos and utilized my tips to get themselves approved for disability benefits.

Having said that, I owe my mother a big debt of gratitude, as well as a thank you, for all of the support and love that has been given over the years with great sacrifice.

Finally, thank you to my in-laws for all that you do for our family, as well as the ongoing love and support.

Avi

About the Author

———

YOU HAVE NEVER MET anyone quite like Avi Leibovic, Esq.

Born in Brooklyn, New York, and raised in Los Angeles, California, **Avi Leibovic** is respected and recognized as one of the most knowledgeable and successful Social Security Disability attorneys in the United States.

In addition, Avi is a community rabbi, social activist, and highly respected orator who has addressed tens of thousands of audience members from various backgrounds and who has developed a reputation for galvanizing audiences with his lively and animated workshops or classes on a myriad of subjects, including, but not limited to, Social Security Disability Law, Jewish History and Philosophy, Family Values, Personal Growth, Character Development, and a special emphasis on "At-Risk" Youth and other sensitive family dynamics.

A former avid heavy metal guitar player, Avi Leibovic has literally gone from "Rocker to Rabbi" and uses his one-of-a-kind stories and personal life experiences to relate to, inspire and call to action the most disenfranchised individuals.

Avi is also a TikTok influencer with over 35 million Tiktok views, over 3000 disability videos online, and over 325,000 dedicated and loyal followers.

In pursuit of his passion for practicing law in the area of public service, Avi is currently the President of **And Benefits for All, LLC**, and the Founding Member of **Avi Leibovic & Associates, PLLC**. His one-of-a-kind Disability Eligibility Program has assisted tens of thousands of disabled individuals to secure their Social Security Disability benefits.

In fact, **And Benefits For All** was selected to receive the prestigious **Legal Elite Award for Best Nationwide Disability Advocacy Firm 2023** from the New World Report, and is one of the recipients of the **2023 National Social Security Disability Leadership Award.**

Avi Leibovic was the Supervising Attorney and Director of the Federal Benefits Department at Health Advocates/Leibovic Law Group from 1998-2016, which assists acute care, public and private hospitals and their indigent and disabled patients in California, apply for Social Security Disability (SSI/SSDI), Medi-Cal, Medicare, Veteran's Affairs (VA), California Children's Services, and other government benefit programs.

During these years at Health Advocates, Avi also successfully coordinated the screening, enrollment, and conversions, as well as all aspects of the Eligibility and Appeals program (including hearings before SSA Administrative Law Judges (ALJ) for over **500,000** disabled individuals.

Avi is an alumnus of Neveh Zion Institute in Israel, Sy Syms School of Business at Yeshiva University New York, City University of New York (CUNY) School of Law, and is admitted to practice law and in good standing with the New York and New Jersey Board of Bar Examiners.

In addition, Rabbi Leibovic received his Rabbinical ordination from Rabbi Mordechai Friedlander of Jerusalem, Israel, in 1998.

In 2001, Avi founded his first not-for-profit organization called **Aish Tamid of Los Angeles**, which has become the primary address and resource within the Los Angeles Orthodox Jewish community for targeted inspiration and personal support for "At-Risk" youth teens and young adults ranging in age between 13 and 28, as well as their families. To date, it has serviced over 5,000 teens, young adults, and their families.

As a result of his work with Aish Tamid, Avi was recognized in 2005 for **Outstanding Community Leadership** through the Community Research and Information Center and received various **Community Leadership** awards from the **United States Senate, the United States House of Congress, California State Assembly, the County of Los Angeles, the City of Los Angeles and the Los Angeles County Sheriff's Department.**

In 2006, Avi was on the cover page of the Los Angeles Jewish Journal as one of the **Top 10 Mensches in Los Angeles**. In January 2007, Aish Tamid was awarded **Best-of-the-Best in Jewish Outreach** by Association of Jewish Outreach Programs (AJOP) in a competitive and international selection process amongst hundreds of national and international organizations.

One of the highlights of Avi's Career, while working and assisting **At-Risk Youth** to find direction, was the creation and founding of **PLAN B High School**.

This one-of-a-kind high school serviced 25 high school drop-out teenagers and was designed specifically to meet the growing needs of the Los Angeles Jewish Community. Each calendar day of the school year was designed to help enhance the individual skills, talents, and abilities of each student. The innovative and cutting-edge PLAN B program delivered education, direction, and guidance in an alternative and intimate setting designed to prevent students from falling through the cracks of larger traditional institutionalized school programs. Each day, the students would meet for religious, spiritual, and group discussions in a setting where they feel comfortable and safe to explore various topics and ask questions about life. On some days, the students would travel by van to specifically selected locations in Los Angeles, wherein trained staff engage the students, run additional individual and group therapy sessions, provide guest speakers, and facilitate the student GED program and community outreach work. Experienced staff will also work with parents at weekly Aish Tamid Parent Forum Groups and offer high-impact Community Workshops on pertinent topics.

In 2012, Avi founded his 2nd and much-needed non-profit organization, **Community Essentials,** in Los Angeles, whose mission is to respectfully, compassionately, and sensitively provide direct assistance to individuals and families in meeting basic survival and living needs.

To date, **Community Essentials** has serviced thousands of requests for assistance within the local Orthodox Jewish community in Los Angeles and New York.

Rabbi Avi Leibovic, Esq. proudly served as the Rabbi and spiritual leader at **Congregation Bais Naftoli in Hancock Park** from 2012-2015.

To date, he has volunteered and provided thousands of hours of one-on-one crisis counseling for students and parents and continues to be a sought-after public speaker at hospitals, county workshops, Jewish synagogues, schools, and community events.

In 2018, Avi moved with his family from California to New York. And, in 2019, opened **AND BENEFITS FOR ALL, LLC** for disability services to the general public on a national scale.

Avi is happily married to his wife, Rena, who is from Long Island, New York, and together they are the proud parents of seven beautiful children, and their growing families.

Together, they make one big happy family!

To contact Avi Leibovic, please visit www.AndBenefitsForAll.com[1].

---

1. http://www.AndBenefitsForAll.com

Introduction

HERE WE ARE.

It's just you and I.

Finally, together and alone at last.

Maybe I should light a candle to keep our conversation personal and intimate? After all, this is a very personal journey you are about to begin.

You are not just holding in your hand a book. You are holding in your hand a roadmap.

A roadmap to where you may ask?

A roadmap that will successfully lead you on your journey towards your destination of getting approved for Social Security Disability Benefits.

Let's be honest with each other, shall we?

You didn't obtain this book to learn how to cook recipes, fix your car, learn history, or read a creative story.

You are reading this book because you desperately need help, encouragement and direction on how to win your claim for Social Security Disability Benefits.

And, guess what…I am going to help you.

Yes, chapter by chapter and tip by tip, I am committed to teaching you everything I know about how to expeditiously and successfully get approved for Social Security disability benefits.

So, let's start from the beginning… I think a little background is in order before we jump into the disability tips.

In 1956, President Dwight D. Eisenhower signed into law the 1956 Amendments to the Social Security Act establishing the Social Security Disability Insurance program.

At first, the program provided monthly benefits only to disabled workers between 50 and 65 years old who met certain requirements for insured status. The age group was later expanded to include benefits for individuals 18 or older.

Although there are several different disability programs: Social Security Disability Insurance (SSDI), Supplemental Security Income (SSI), Disabled Adult Child, or Disabled Widow(er)'s Benefits, this book is only going to specifically address:

Social Security Disability Insurance, also known as SSDI, and **Supplemental Security Income, also known as SSI** — These are two very different programs with very different eligibility criteria.

I always like to compare these programs to the prizes you can receive at the local county fair games. As you know, when you play a game at the county fair, you can usually win two different types of prizes — the big stuffed teddy bear or the little stuffed teddy bear. I think you would agree that you always want to win the bigger teddy bear. The bigger teddy bear can be compared to the SSDI program.

SSDI is a larger and more robust program that offers you more benefits if you are approved.

On the other hand, SSI also awards you a benefits package, but it is not as big or as substantial.

To quote www.ssa.gov[2], the Social Security Administration web page, *"The SSDI program pays benefits to you and certain family members that are "insured." This means that you worked long enough — and recently enough — and paid Social Security taxes on your earnings.*

The SSI program pays benefits to adults and children who meet the requirements for a qualifying disability and have limited income and resources.

While these two programs are different, the medical requirements are the same. If you meet the nonmedical requirements, monthly benefits are paid if you have a medical condition expected to last at least one year or result in death."

SSDI, generally, requires you to have 40 active work credits. www.ssa.gov[3] continues to say, "*Social Security work credits are based on your total yearly wages or self-employment income. You can earn up to four credits each year.*

The amount needed for a work credit changes from year to year. In 2023, for example, you earn one credit for each $1,640 in wages or self-employment income. When you've earned $6,560, you've earned your four credits for the year.

The number of work credits you need to qualify for disability benefits depends on your age when your disability begins.

Generally, you need 40 credits, 20 of which were earned in the last 10 years ending with the year your disability begins. However, younger workers may qualify with fewer credits."

SSI, on the other hand, "*provides monthly payments to adults and children with a disability or blindness who have income[4] and resources[5] below specific financial limits. SSI payments are also made to people aged 65 and older without disabilities who meet the financial qualifications.*

You may be eligible to receive SSI monthly payments even if you are already receiving Social Security Disability Insurance or retirement benefits."

Additionally, in most states, an SSI recipient will automatically qualify for health care coverage through Medicaid. A person with SSDI, on the other hand, will automatically qualify for Medicare after 24 months of receiving disability payments. All of this will be discussed at length in different chapters in this book. Don't worry; I've got you covered.

So back to the teddy bear example.

---

3. http://www.ssa.gov

4. *https://www.ssa.gov/ssi/text-income-ussi.htm*

5. *https://www.ssa.gov/ssi/text-resources-ussi.htm*

The reason I compare SSDI to the large stuffed teddy bear, as opposed to SSI, which is the smaller stuffed teddy bear, is because SSDI has several major differences from SSI. For starters (and all of this will be discussed later):

1. SSDI allows you to go retroactive one (1) year from the application date. That means that if you are just now learning about SSDI, but you have already been out of work for a year because of your medical condition(s), you can go backwards one (1) year on the application date to collect one year of payments. SSI only allows you to collect benefits from the application date forward.

2. SSDI will award additional benefits to your insured family members, namely your unmarried children under 18 who are still in school. These are called "Auxiliary benefits." SSI, on the other hand, has no awards for children of disabled beneficiaries.

3. As briefly mentioned above, SSDI awards you Medicare after 24 months from your Entitlement date, while SSI (in most states) only awards Medicaid. This is a big one for those of you who are desperately trying to get medical attention and medication that you so desperately need.

4. The SSDI benefit amount is based on your earnings and what you paid into the system over the course of your working career. SSI is a flat state amount, and everyone in your state usually gets the same amount. This can be a substantial difference in the dollar amount paid to you and is probably the biggest difference between SSDI and SSI.

5. SSDI allows you to apply online at www.ssa.gov[6], while SSI only allows a paper application at this time. You can begin the SSI process online, but you will have to complete it with your local SSA District Office.

6. SSI will count your spouse/partner's income and resources when you apply to make sure you are within the eligibility limits. With SSDI, your spouse/partner's income and resources have no bearing on your claim for benefits.

Of course, some of this may be confusing to you, but I am confident that by the time you work your way thru the 101 disability tips that are in this book, you will become a master at how to maneuver the Social Security Disability process.

---

6. http://www.ssa.gov

Yes, the facts of each disability case are different and the strategies employed to navigate and win a case will always be depended on the unique facts and circumstances in each case. But these essential tips will apply to most, if not all, of you.

From the bottom of my heart, I want to congratulate you on taking the first step toward helping yourself win your case.

I know in my heart that these tips work. I have been successfully using them for over 25 years.

The most important tip that I can give you is to hire an attorney to help you win your case!!! You will thank me later.

Additionally, since there is NO attorney-client relationship that exists between you and I, it is essential that you hire an attorney who can become intimately familiar with your case and navigate you accordingly based on the facts of your circumstances.

You have nothing to lose. Disability attorneys will NOT charge you for their services, unless they win your claim for benefits. Having an experienced and educated attorney on your side can make all the difference, especially at the time of the hearing.

***** **It should also be noted that these tips are in NO PARTICULAR ORDER OF IMPORTANCE. They can be read in the order of chapters 1 to 101, or in any order you wish. They are all timely, relevant and important.** *****

When I was a younger boy, I always had in my head the image of Rocky Balboa, the movie character, who raised his hands in victory after defeating his opponent and then screamed out, "*WE DID IT*!!!"

I want nothing more than for you to also raise your hands in victory after winning your disability case and have you dancing around your house while screaming, "*WE DID IT*!!!"

You CAN do it. I believe in you.

— Avi

Tip #1: 12 or More Months

ACCORDING TO THE SOCIAL Security Administration, the word "Disability" is defined as *"the inability to engage in any substantial gainful activity (SGA) by reason of any medically determinable physical or mental impairment(s) which can be expected to result in death or which has lasted or can be expected to last for a continuous period of not less than 12 months."*

The question becomes, how do we understand the words *"which has lasted or can be expected to last for a continuous period of not less than 12 months?"* This becomes a critical part of determining whether or not you will win your Social Security Disability claim for benefits.

For example, if someone were to go skiing and were to break their ankle while skiing, would they be considered disabled?

The answer to that question depends on whether or not the broken ankle will prevent the person from returning to their old job or getting any other job with the national economy where they earn more than Substantial Gainful Activity (SGA) for a continuous 12-month period. In most cases, a broken ankle will heal before the 12-month period is met. So, therefore, the person will not be considered "disabled."

Let's take another example of somebody who may have recently been diagnosed with cancer. This person will clearly require multiple treatments, possibly chemotherapy and/or radiation, and the patient may potentially be in and out of the hospital several times. He or she will most probably, be out of work for 12 or more months. Even though you can say that it hasn't been 12 or more months since the cancer was diagnosed, we all know that cancer or the lingering impact of cancer *"can be expected to last for a continuous period of not less than 12 months."*

Having said that, this person will meet the durational criteria and hopefully be found to be medically disabled by the Social Security Administration.

This 12-month durational requirement doesn't just apply to physical conditions, but it also applies the mental conditions like Depression, Anxiety, Post-Traumatic Stress Disorder, etc.

The question to be answered is whether or not a mental impairment or combination of mental impairments such as Depression, Anxiety, or Post-Traumatic Stress Disorder *"can be expected to last for a continuous period of not less than 12 months?"*

In most cases, you will have to show and establish with your medical records that you've either been treated by a psychiatrist, psychologist, or a therapist for at least 12 or more months and that the condition is so severe that it's going to last *"for a continuous period of not less than 12 months."*

The basic conclusion is that if you want to win your Social Security claim, it's **not** just about having a medical condition. Rather, it is about having a medical condition that will last or is expected to last for 12 or more months and which prevents you from returning to your old job or performing any other job in the national economy.

Over the years, I've received phone calls from clients who want to apply for disability benefits, but are unclear about this 12-month criteria. For instance, they may have pulled their back, or they may have some other ailment(s) that recently started affecting their body. I immediately have to ask them if their medical condition will last for *"a continuous period of not less than 12 months?"* If they do not expect it to last for 12 or more months, then they have no chance of winning their claim for benefits.

It isn't just about having 12 or more months of disability. But, it's about having a ***severe*** impairment where you cannot earn income or where you cannot engage in any activity, which is called "Substantial Gainful Activity" or "SGA," for short. The Social Security Administration defines SGA by a specific dollar amount each year. That dollar amount is the maximum amount of money that you can earn each month in order to determine if you are working or not.

In 2020, SGA was $1,220 per month, and in 2021 SGA was $1,310 per month. In 2022, SGA was $1,350 per month, and in 2023 the SGA amount has been increased to $1,470 per month. Note: the SGA dollar amounts are higher for blind individuals. Having said that, it isn't just about having a medical condition for 12 months. Rather, it's about having a medical condition for 12 or more months, where you are unable to engage in SGA.

Suppose you are earning more than SGA for even one of the 12 consecutive months. Generally, in that case, you are not going to be eligible for Social Security disability benefits. Anytime you earn over the SGA amounts, you disqualify yourselves from the 12 or more months criteria to be found eligible for Social Security disability benefits.

The first important tip to remember is that in order to win your Social Security claim, you must have a severe medical condition that is expected to last for "*a continuous period of not less than 12 months*," which has prevented you from earning SGA during that time period.

Without those 12 durational months, you cannot win your case — ever!

Tip #2: Never Lie to the Judge

AT ONE POINT OR ANOTHER in life, we may find ourselves in a situation where we have to go to court and face a Judge.

As we all know, whenever you go to court, you must take an oath to tell the truth, the whole truth, and nothing but the truth.

For some reason, people don't seem to take that rule to heart, and they find themselves either exaggerating the truth, embellishing the truth, or stretching the truth when the time comes to give testimony to the Judge.

This becomes especially important in a disability case since the Judge must take your testimony in order to determine if you are disabled or not. In all cases, the testimony will have to match up with the objective medical evidence in the record, meaning you have to let your doctors and your hospitals document all of your medical conditions and symptoms in the medical record. The Judge is going to match up all of your testimony with the medical records and the notes in the medical records.

Every person needs to understand that Judges spend their entire day listening to the testimony of the people who stand before them at trial. Having said that, Judges have become experts in differentiating between those telling the truth versus those who are not telling the truth. Other examples of giving testimony to a Judge don't necessarily involve medical conditions or symptoms, but the testimony can also include actions taken by a person during the course of a day called "Activities of Daily Living" or "ADLs."

For instance, you will have to give testimony regarding whether or not you can get out of bed each morning, walk to the bathroom, dress, shower and bath, purchase foods or other household items, prepare meals, do the laundry, make the beds, wash the floors, etc. These are simple examples of ADLs.

Claimants often tell the Judge that they're unable to perform their Activities of Daily Living under any circumstances because of their restrictions and limitation relating to their medical conditions. Unfortunately, they're also on social media posting that they're performing many different types of strenuous activities during the same time period, and they're claiming that they're disabled. Alternatively, the medical records make no mention of any of these restrictions or limitations.

They may have also recently gone on vacation and enjoyed jet skiing, scuba diving, hiking, or any other type of strenuous activity, and they reported this to their medical providers. The Judges, if they want, can go online to social media and verify this information. They can also scan your medical records to see what was reported to your doctors. Suppose they find that your stories do not match up, meaning that the testimony you are giving in court under oath doesn't match up with what you're posting on social media. In that case, your credibility will be ruined, and you will lose your case.

So, it is essential to always tell the truth to the Judge, whether discussing your medical conditions or discussing any ADL actions taken. You must never lie to a Judge.

If the Judge finds or catches you in the lie, your credibility will be destroyed. And you will lose your case in almost every instance since you can no longer be trusted.

One area that comes up a lot and is a source of difficulty for many individuals is the issue of street drugs and alcohol. How often or when was the last time non-prescribed drugs were used? When was the last time alcohol was consumed? What were the quantities that were used? When did you become sober? How long did the drug and alcohol continue?

These are very important items that a Judge needs to know and that a Judge looks carefully at when determining whether or not to grant disability benefits. You cannot lie to a Judge under any circumstances ever!

I once had a case where the gentleman used to be a mechanic and fix cars. He told the Judge that he had not been able to work for the last 12 or more months because the injuries on his back prevented him from moving around and fixing the cars.

After a few more minutes of testimony, the Judge leaned over the bench and asked the gentleman to raise his hands for a closer inspection. When the gentleman raised his hands, it was clear to the whole court that there were oil smudges on his fingertips and that his hands were tough, rough, and calloused. The skin was cracked because of the work he had recently been performing on vehicles.

Even though in his testimony to the Judge, he stated that he wasn't working, his hands proved otherwise. This example shows that you could never lie to the Judge under any circumstances. What was the Judge's verdict? That person lost their case.

The moral of the story is: *Never lie to the Judge!*

Tip #3: The Key is Medical Records

THE MOST IMPORTANT evidence in any disability case is the medical records.

Whether these are records from a local doctor, an urgent care center, a specialist, or a hospital. Your medical records will determine whether or not you will win your disability case.

A good doctor will make sure that they document everything you tell them and everything that they see with their own eyes in the medical records. A good doctor will make sure that every symptom is notated in the charts, every laboratory test is included in the records, and every imaging result is included in the complete medical records.

Unfortunately, some doctors do not take their job as seriously as other doctors or are careless at what they do and they do not completely document the medical records based on what you're telling them. Shame on them!

This happens almost daily. When a person goes to their doctor and starts describing their symptoms and their ailments to the doctor, you will often find that the doctor is simply nodding their head in agreement or affirmatively receiving the information but not necessarily documenting the medical records.

People don't realize that with the Social Security Administration, medical evaluators have to review these medical records many months after these people have visited the doctor. If the doctor does not properly document the medical records with everything that the patient says, then when the Social Security medical evaluators (or the disability Judge) reviews the medical records, there will be a problem.

Why?

Because the doctor was just listening instead of actively writing down the statements of the patient, the essential aspects of the diagnosis, resulting in essential symptoms and items missing from the medical records.

In essence, you have a broad overview of diagnosis, but you're missing the specific narratives and specific characteristics of the ailments. Broad overviews by a doctor relating to a general diagnosis will never win a case for Social Security disability benefits.

Social Security loves details! Social Security loves specifics! Social Security loves descriptions relating to medical conditions!

So, if your doctor is not writing down these items, you stand a good chance of struggling to win your case or even losing your case.

Great advice that I tell all my clients is that when they go to the doctor and notice that the doctor is not writing down any of their symptoms or comments in the notes, they should respectfully tell the doctor that they're applying for disability benefits. Furthermore, that the Social Security Administration is going to want to know all the facts. You need to tell the doctor that you would appreciate it if the doctor would begin to notate all of the medical records with everything that is being reported to him or her.

This is specifically true and of utmost importance when it comes to issues of pain and determining not only how much pain a person is in, but also the duration of the pain, the frequency of the pain, as well as the location of the pain.

Doctors must write everything down, especially when dealing with mental health cases, as well.

This is also the case when patients visit their psychologists or their therapists and engage in "talk" therapy. As all of us know, or as many of us have experienced, when you go to a therapist or psychologist for an hour's appointment, you tell them everything about yourself.

The question is, how much is your therapist or psychologist writing down? When dealing with a specific diagnosis like depression, anxiety, schizophrenia, or post-traumatic stress disorder, the details are extremely important. Judges want to know, and Social Security wants to know:

- How often do you have crying spells;

- Whether or not you can sleep at night;

- Whether or not there's been an increase or decrease in weight;

- If you're having anxiety attacks;

- How often do you tend to have anxiety attacks;

- If you're isolated in your home and are afraid to go out in public;

- If you are able to engage in activities of daily living, including cooking, bathing, and shopping;

- Whether or not you have thoughts of suicide and/or of hurting yourself or other people;

- Can you engage with the public;

- What are your sleeping habits;

- Do you hear voices or see things;

- And many more details....

All of these items must be written down and recorded in the medical records if you want to win a mental health case. You probably will not win your case without these fine details noted in the medical records.

It is worthwhile to also mention now that your therapy session notes need to be released to SSA for review. I have had many clients whose therapists refused to release the session notes because of the confidentiality related to these records. That's just nonsense. Everything released to your attorney and/or SSA is protected information. It must be released to SSA in order for them to decide your case.

Whether your medical condition is physical or mental, the key is to have medical records that have few gaps, if any.

Do not let too many months pass before you go to get a check-up from your doctor.

Keep your medical appointments.

Make sure that your medical provider is writing everything down in your medical records.

We don't want to leave anything to chance.

It must all be documented!

Tip #4: Always Call Back Your Attorney

PEOPLE SPEND A LOT of time trying to find the best attorney to represent them in a disability case before the Social Security Administration.

To find the best attorney, they often ask their friends for their experiences with attorneys, they look on the internet to see if they can read reviews about an attorney, and they heavily rely on feedback given to them by family as to whether or not an attorney is a good attorney and competent to represent them before the Social Security Administration.

After taking so much time to find the right attorney, and after beginning to work with the attorney to give them the names of their doctors and medications, as well as describing to them all the aspects of your case, many people don't realize that the attorney jumps into action, and right away begins to work your claim for benefits.

Additionally, the attorney will contact the local SSA District Office for you, contact the Disability Determination Services, contact all of your doctors to make sure they're sending in medical records, contact the Office of Hearings and Operations, and make sure the Judge's electronic exhibit file is up to date. Besides the above, they will perform a host of other actions on your behalf.

But every now and then, the attorney needs *your* help in order to obtain certain information that is extremely important to the case. They may need a date that you received a letter from SSA or if that letter has a denial date on it. They may need the telephone number of a doctor or the address of a hospital. They may need to schedule a hearing with a Judge, and they want to make sure that you are free on that day.

So, what does the attorney do? The attorney calls you up on your telephone and tries to get in touch with you to get the needed information so that the attorney can respond timely. Unfortunately, for many different reasons, they get your voicemail and leave a voice message for you to call them back.

It boggles my mind, and I'm at a loss of words; how many times in my career I've left a message for one of my clients and did not receive a telephone call back. Doesn't the client understand that I'm working on their behalf to win a case? Doesn't the client understand that I'm under time constraints and that I need to provide essential information to the Social Security Administration and or to the Judge? Doesn't the client understand that I'm not calling them for my benefit, but I'm calling them for *their* own benefit?

I simply don't understand why the client sometimes doesn't call the attorney back. This is especially the case when there is a hearing approaching. The attorney must prepare the client for the upcoming hearing. Any good attorney will spend a minimum of 45-60 minutes in the days leading up to the hearing just preparing the clients for every aspect of a case before a Judge.

They will describe to them what to expect at the hearing in this preparation; they will describe to them that they will be a part of the hearing; if there will be any experts that will be called or not; they will describe in the preparation the merits of the case and the strength of the case so that the client is fully prepared for the hearing and feels confident going into the hearing that they've been prepared. So, what happens when the attorney calls the clients to prepare them for the hearing, but the client doesn't call back?

When the client does not call back after spending having spent 12 or 18 to 24 months working on a case, the client is not going to be prepared for the questions that the Judge will ask. The client is not well-versed in how to respond to the questions. And the client is confused as to how the hearing is conducted.

In most cases, a client who doesn't call his attorney back before a hearing will probably lose his case before the Judge since they will not understand the mechanics of the hearing, as well as the attorney strategies used in the hearing to win the case.

In short, there is a partnership that is formed between you and your attorney, and I will keep emphasizing that over and over again in this book. Both the attorney and the client have to work hand-in-hand to win the case.

Please stay in contact with your attorney at least every 30 days, so you can be up-to-date on all the aspects of your case.

Additionally, if you change your phone number or change your address, make sure that you call your attorney and let them know the changes you have made so your attorney can be up to date and can contact you when they need you.

Bottom line, always call your attorney back!

Tip #5: Don't Forget to Take Your Medication

THERE ARE A LOT OF pieces to the puzzle to help you win a Social Security Disability case. Your age, education, past relevant work, and medical conditions are only part of the puzzle. Additionally, the treatment you receive, who your SSA/DDS Case Manager is, and the amount of time it takes for your doctors to send in those medical records are also pieces of the puzzle that have to be considered when determining the success of your case.

Overlooked aspects, which are very important to Judges and the Social Security Administration, are whether or not you take your medications regularly as prescribed by your doctor. I cannot tell you how many times in my career I have stood before a Judge, and the Judge asked the client the following questions:

- Do you take your medications?

- Do you take your medications daily?

- Do you take your medications as prescribed by the doctor?

Unfortunately, the client will get flustered at these questions if they weren't prepared for them and then sits there and lies to the Judge and says yes to the questions. They lie about taking the medications as prescribed by their doctor.

The problem is that the Judge knows that the client is lying. How do the Judges know when the Claimant is lying? Because the doctor wrote in the medical records whether or not the patient is following and compliant with prescribed medication regimens. When a doctor writes over many months and several times in the records that you "failed to comply" with your medication regimens, the Social Security Administration, medical evaluators, and doctors, as well as the Judges, do not look favorably upon your case.

As we said above, many pieces of the puzzle help you win your case. Taking your medications regularly is a very important one. Taking medication daily is one of the most important and overlooked puzzle pieces that must be considered when determining the success of a Social Security disability case.

This doesn't only apply to medications. This also applies to other aspects of medical treatments that have been prescribed by the doctor, including but not limited to injections, physical therapy, occupational therapy, stretching, and regular attendance to upcoming medical appointments. An exception can be made if a patient opts NOT to have a specific or dangerous surgery, as no Judge can force you to have surgery. But, besides this exception, don't expect to win your case if you're not doing your part to help yourself feel better.

It goes without mentioning that you should be taking your medications because you need your medications and not because you're trying to win your Social Security case. You should be taking your medications because you're trying to live a healthy and long life. Your medications that have been prescribed to you by your doctor are there to help you accomplish that goal. When you fail to take your medications, not only do you not feel well, but you will also decrease your chances of ever getting better and or maintaining a normal healthy lifestyle.

Disability tip number Five is to **Always take your medication.**

Tip #6: Don't Miss
Your Consultative Examination

AFTER FILING YOUR APPLICATION with the local SSA District Office, part of your application will be sent to the Disability Determination Services (DDS), which is part of your State Department of Rehabilitation, for review of the medical aspects of the case.

Many people don't realize this, but the local SSA District Office has nothing to do with the medical reviews related to your disability case.

The local SSA District Offices are more concerned with the non-medical administrative aspects of your case. They are concerned with answers to questions like:

- Are you a US citizen?

- Are you a resident of the state?

- Are you currently working and earning over SGA?

- Do you have enough active work credits for SSDI?

- Is your spouse earning too much income?

- Are you receiving any unearned income?

- Do you have too many resources which exclude you from eligibility? Etc.

The Social Security District Office has nothing to do with the medical determinations. Only DDS makes the decision on the medical aspects of your case. Sometimes, even though your medical records have been provided to the Social Security Administration or the DDS, there is not enough information in the medical records to determine whether or not you are disabled.

As such, DDS will almost always schedule a Consultative Examination (CE) for you with one of the contracted DDS local doctors. This can either be a physical Consultative Examination, a mental Consultative Examination, or a specialty examination based on certain ailments that you have identified in your Social Security Administration case.

Attending Consultant Examinations is not optional; it is not voluntary. It is not at your discretion to attend or not to attend; it is mandatory if you want to win your case!

Throughout the course of my career, I cannot tell you how many times people have lost their cases simply because they didn't attend their consultative examination.

The Consultative Examination usually lasts between 20 minutes and 45 minutes. It is usually a simple examination from your head to your toes, internal and external. It is not a comprehensive full-blown examination.

The doctors who examine you generally note down everything that you do and everything that you say. The doctors notate in the reports whether you drove to the examination in your own car and/or if anybody accompanied you. They are watching to see if you're able to jump on and off of the table on your own, without difficulty, if you're able to dress and undress without difficulty if you're able to walk and stand without support and difficulty. What is your range of motion with the different parts of your body? Everything is being written and noted down. If you fail to attend your consultative examination, you put at risk the chance of winning your case.

When you attend your CE, here is what you should make sure you tell the examiner: (1) all of your medical conditions, (2) all of your medications (write them down on a piece of paper!), (3) the names of any hospitals you were admitted to in the last 2 years, and most importantly (4) all of your medical symptoms (yes, ALL of them!)

You must get it all on paper since DDS (and the Judge (if you have to go to a hearing)) WILL be looking at the summary of that examination. If something important relating to your medical impairments isn't written on that examination summary, then DDS or the Judge won't know this crucial information.

My advice, if you cannot attend your Consultative Examination, is to call up your DDS analyst who's working on your case. You must be able to provide a "good cause" reason you are unable to attend the examination so that the Consultative Examination can be rescheduled. I cannot emphasize enough how important that Consultative Examination is for the success of your case.

Tip #7: Preparing for Your Hearing

THE FIRST STEP IN BEGINNING your claim for disability benefits is the initial application.

According to the released national data by SSA, there is approximately a 70% denial rate for initial Applications. The next step, if your application is denied, is a Request for Reconsideration.

According to the most recent national data, Requests for Reconsiderations have a 15% reversal rate. This means that 85% of the denied cases at the Reconsideration level will be eligible for an actual disability hearing before an Administrative Law Judge.

The waiting time for a hearing before an Administrative Law Judge can be anywhere from 8 months to 12 months, depending on the state that you live in.

Although the Social Security Administration is working as diligently as it can to shorten that waiting period, at some point, your hearing date will come up on the calendar. You need to be in touch with your attorney as your hearing date approaches.

Not only do you need to update your attorney with any new medical providers (so that the records can be requested), but you need to also prepare yourself for the hearing! What is really essential is that you're in touch with your attorney one or two days before your hearing so that you can have your attorney prepare you for all aspects of the hearing before you go in front of the Judge.

In my experience, unless a client is prepared for all aspects of the hearing, he or she runs a good chance of losing their case to the Administrative Law Judge. Any good attorney knows that they must spend anywhere from 45 to 60 minutes, at a minimum, preparing their clients for the hearing. It is not uncommon to practice 200-250 sample questions that the Judge may ask the client so that they are prepared, confident, relaxed, and understand how the hearing process works.

If they want their client to win, there are many aspects to a hearing, and it is the attorney's obligation and duty to make sure that the client is prepared and familiar with all aspects of what will occur in the hearing. Most hearings all follow the same format.

Each hearing will begin with the Judge confirming some personal background information about the Claimants, such as:

- Address

- Telephone number

- Date of birth

- Social Security number

The Judge will usually also confirm other essential background information like their height, weight, education level, whether they are right-handed or left-handed, whether they have any military experience, and/or if they have a driver's license and are using their car regularly. That is usually the first introductory part of the hearing.

The next part of the hearing generally will include information on past relevant work history. The Social Security Administration can go and look at the last 15 years of your past relevant work history to determine what type of jobs you've had and what you have done in your career.

Here, they will look at the length of time you worked at a job, the titles that you had at that job, the duties and responsibilities you performed on the job, how much you were paid at that job as well as the length of time you were employed at that job. If you were a Manager or Supervisor, they would also look to see if your responsibilities included hiring and firing and/or processing payroll, vacation, and sick time.

They are trying to determine what skills you have and if those skills are transferable to any other jobs in the national economy. Remember, the whole point of the hearing is to determine whether or not you can be employed in the national economy at either your old job or any other job. Identifying the past relevant work history you have helps the Judge decide if you can return to your old job or whether you can get any other job in the national economy.

The Judge will also have a brief conversation with your attorney regarding the medical records in the Exhibit File. Have all the medical records and other exhibits been submitted? Is the record complete, or does the Judge need to hold the record open for another 14-30 days until additional records or documents come in?

Thereafter, the Judge will generally ask you about your medical conditions which are preventing you from working. They will ask you to describe in your own words why you feel you're unable to work. The attorney must prepare the clients for properly answering this question with the most effective type of answers that go directly to the point. The attorney must also remind the client that the Judge is not looking for long narratives or long stories but prefers short, detailed, straight-to-the-point answers to the questions.

Since it is very common that people usually have many medical conditions, I usually like to coach my clients and remind them that when they are describing their medical conditions at the beginning of the hearing to the Judge, that they should either start from their head, move down their body toward their toes, or start from their toes and move up towards their head. Thereafter, they should work from the inside of their body to the outside of their body. Meaning if you're working from the head down, you may want to describe to the Judge that you have headaches or that you have problems with your vision. When I recommend going from the inside of the body to the outside of the body, I am talking about medical conditions that cannot be seen by the eye – Lupus, Diabetes, Fibromyalgia, etc.

Thereafter, you may describe that you have neck pain. Thereafter, you may describe some of the issues you have with your shoulders, your arms or your elbows or your wrists, or your fingers. You may discuss if you have a limited range of motion or swelling. Continuing down the body, you may want to talk about your chest and any pains you have with breathing. You can discuss the pains you have with your heart, continuing down your body; you may think they want to go ahead and talk about any difficulties you have with your spine and your back.

And then continuing down to your waist, your hips, knees, ankles, and toes, slowly and methodically working down your body to make sure that you haven't forgotten any parts of your body that are causing you ailments and preventing you from working.

Of course, don't forget that we then need to work from the inside out, which means that you may want to talk about things that are not visible to the eye, at least on the first inspection, like high blood pressure or high sugar levels in your blood or other items which cannot be easily seen by the eye and or which require imaging, lab tests, or radiology reports in order to ascertain the severity of the medical condition. Autoimmune conditions, neurological and other "invisible conditions" need to also be discussed at length with the Judge.

Finally, if you have any mental health issues, such as schizophrenia, anxiety or depression, borderline personality disorders, post-traumatic stress disorders, etc., that would be a good time to discuss how those medical conditions impact you. We will have a chapter later on in this book to discuss at length how to describe all the different symptoms of mental health issues and ailments you might have.

Medications and their side effects are also something that a client needs to be made aware of because he will have to give testimony on that before the Judge at the hearing. The attorney must prepare the client to make sure that the client is ready to discuss the medications he takes, the dosage amounts, the frequency, and the side effects of the medications.

Generally, there are three absolute rules relating to a hearing that is done by telephone or by zoom-teleconference:

- The first rule for a telephone or video hearing is that you must be alone in a room by yourself;

- The second rule is that you cannot record the hearing proceedings and that the court will make an official recording;

- The third rule is that the Judges ideally do not want you referencing any notes or any papers and that your testimony is your alone, without any help or assistance from any third party, including by text-messages.

Testimony during the hearing will also include aspects of Activities of Daily Living or "ADLs." The Judge will want to know what time you get up in the morning, do you need assistance in getting out of bed, do you need help in getting dressed or bathing/showering, or taking care of any other hygienic needs. The Judge will also want to know if you're able to cook for yourself and shop for food, as well as perform any other chores in the house like washing dishes, vacuuming, cleaning the beds, or doing laundry or comment if you need someone else to assist and support you with these activities of daily living.

The Judge will want to know how you spend your free time during the day, whether you travel in and out of a home, as well as if you attend the church, synagogue, or mosque regularly.

Finally, toward the end of the hearing, the Judge may take testimony from a Medical Expert (ME) or a Vocational Expert (VE). It should be noted that the Judge does not have to listen to the Medical Expert or the Vocational Expert's testimony as the final say in a matter but that they are going to give their expert opinion to the Judge.

Nevertheless, the attorney needs to prepare the clients and explain to them the role of the Medical Experts and the Vocational Experts and what their testimony will entail over the next few minutes of the hearing periods. The Medical Expert is there to explain any of the medical conditions to the Judge, to explain any of the side effects that the medications may have to the Judge, and most importantly, to tell the Judge if the medical conditions being alleged by the Claimant to meet or equal one of the Social Security Adult Listings and/or Rulings or Regulations. (There will be a chapter later on in this book about Social Security Adult Listings and Regulations).

The Vocational Expert, on the other hand, is there to give their expert testimony as to whether or not a hypothetical individual who has the same age, education, and exertional limitations as you can perform any of the past work that you performed or if they can get any other job in the national economy. The attorney should prepare the client to let them know that in almost every case, the Vocational Expert will be able to find at least three (3) jobs that the hypothetical Claimant can perform. Whether or not YOU specifically are able to perform these jobs, in actuality, is irrelevant! After all, these are hypothetical questions that the Judge asks the Vocational Experts. All that matters is whether or not the expert is able to find any other type of job which he believes the Claimant can perform in the national economy. It is then the attorney's job to chisel away at those jobs listed by the Vocational Expert and to get the Vocational Expert down to zero jobs.

There are many ways to accomplish this task, and a skilled courtroom attorney should know all of the legal techniques in order to effectively cross-examine the Vocational Expert.

In general, the easiest and best way to get the Vocational Expert down to zero jobs is if the attorney asks the Expert if the hypothetical person with the same age, education, and background as the Claimant will be "off-task" more than 10% of the time or be absent from work more than 2-3 times a month.

The answer to each of these questions will always result in an erosion of jobs and the unavailability of any jobs in the national economy, bringing the Vocational Expert witness to admit that there are zero jobs available in the national economy.

Finally, it is also the attorney's job to prepare the Claimant with some sort of emotional closing statement as to why the Judge should approve their claim for benefits.

As you can see, there's quite a bit of preparation that is required by the attorney and by the Claimant prior to the hearing. Any attorney who does not take the time to prepare their clients for the hearing is doing a tremendous disservice to their clients and runs a good chance of them losing their claim.

In my career, after performing 1000's of hearings, I have found that the biggest indicator of success in a case (besides the quality of the medical records) is the preparation of the Claimant before appearing in front of the Judge at the hearing.

With the proper preparation, every attorney should go over at least 90% to 95% of all the questions that the Judge can potentially ask the Claimant at the hearing.

By the time the attorney is done preparing the client for the hearing, the client should be calm, confident, and have high aspirations about performing well at the hearing about winning their case. You must always prepare for the hearing!

Tip #8: Updating Your SSA District Office

WHEN LOOKING AT OUR country from "sea to shining sea," it quickly becomes evident that the United States of America is very large.

It has to be divided up, at first, region by region, then state by state, county by county, city by city, and district by district.

Just like every neighborhood has a post office, police and fire station, each neighborhood also has a local SSA District Office that is there to service all of their Social Security needs. If you want to find your local District Office, all you need to do is go to Google and search for "SSA office locator" (or go to www.ssa.gov[1]), and Boom! You will easily find your neighborhood SSA District Office.

This search will pull up results of your local SSA District Office address, the office telephone number, as well as the fax number. It is the responsibility of the local District Office to service all your SSA needs, and your local District Office has jurisdiction over your claim for benefits once they are filed with the Social Security Administration.

Basically, the District Office is your home base. You will need their help to help process your claim for benefits. As such, you must update the Social Security Administration if you move to a new neighborhood so that they can update their databases to make sure that not only do they have your new address and telephone numbers, but to make sure that the case is also being moved from one SSA District office to the new SSA District office so that the new office has jurisdiction to work your case.

Many people don't realize that the SSA District office serves several functions as it relates to a disability claim. Some of the functions they perform have to do with confirming the following:

---

1. http://www.ssa.gov

- If you have enough active work credits to file a Social Security Disability Insurance Benefits claim;

- If you meet the citizenship requirements for benefits;

- If you meet the residency requirements;

- If you have too much income or too many other resources;

- And other administrative functions.

The SSA District Office does not determine if you are medically disabled or not. That job belongs to the Disability Determination Services (DDS). But, the District office does complete the review for all other aspects of the case. Having said that, once again, if you move, you must notify your local SSA District office of your move.

Not only will you continue to receive your mail relating to your claim, but the District Office will make sure that the proper jurisdiction is given to the proper SSA District Office. The last thing you want is for your file or claim to fall into a dark black hole or the SSA system 'cracks.' To prevent your case from falling into the cracks of the system and into a black hole, you must update the District Office if you move.

Your local District Office will also be able to tell you how much your monthly benefits amount will be once you are approved for benefits. This is called your "Primary Insurance Amount" or "PIA."

The SSA District Office will also generate an Award Letter if you are approved (or a denial letter if you are denied), which will contain a complete breakdown as to when your benefits start, how much you will be getting each month, what the full benefit backpay amount will be, and how much needs to be paid to your attorney if you have one. The Award Letter will also contain information about either Medicaid or Medicare, depending if you were approved for SSI and/or SSDI.

As such, you must keep your local SSA District Office up-to-date with your most recent address and telephone number so that you can continue to receive all of the SSA notices that are sent to your home. Your failure to update SSA with this information will almost certainly result in you missing important and critical information related to your claim for benefits.

As of August 2023, many of the local SSA District Offices remain closed due the extraordinary circumstances stemming from the COVID-19 Pandemic.

While some District Offices are open for business, others are still closed or operating at reduced hours with most of the staff still working remotely.

As such, I would highly recommend that you do not just travel down to your local SSA District Office without first calling them or looking on-line at www.ssa.gov[2] to confirm if they are open.

---

2. http://www.ssa.gov

Tip #9: Calling Your SSA District Office

DO YOU LIKE PUZZLES? What about games? How about mazes?

Well, at times, it may seem like the Social Security Administration can be a big maze or labyrinth.

For those of you who are unfamiliar with how the process of applying for benefits works, it can definitely feel like you are in some sort of strange game with no idea of how to win.

Not only are there many SSA forms that need to be filled out during the eligibility and/or appeal process, but there also are many different personalities and offices that are involved in the processing of your claims, like the SSA District Office, Disability Determination Services, the Office of Hearings and Operations, and the Payment Center.

In order to start a claim for benefits, you must begin with an initial application. This initial application can be filed online at www.ssa.gov[1], by paper or over the telephone, depending on your preference.

Within a few weeks of filing your claim for benefits, your case will be assigned to a local SSA District Office in order to begin processing your case. Once it's assigned to a local SSA District Office, it will also be assigned to a Social Security Case Manager within that SSA District Office. Please be patient; depending on the District Office backlog, this can take a few days, weeks, or months for this first assignment step to occur.

Each Social Security case manager is assigned hundreds of cases to work on their inventory list.

---

1. http://www.ssa.gov

For each of those cases, there is a multitude of tasks that need to be performed. These include reviewing work credits, citizenship requirements, residency requirements, income and resource requirements, as well as other jurisdictional aspects of the case.

Remember, the SSA District office doesn't perform the medical review of your case, as that task is for the Disability Determination Services (DDS). Nevertheless, your case cannot progress toward approval without the hands-on assistance of the Social Security worker at your local District office.

So, what is the best advice that I can give you in order to make sure that your case is processed timely? The answer is very simple, but it's often overlooked. The answer is to pick up the phone and call the Social Security District Office and introduce yourself. Make sure they have everything they need from you.

Social Security Administration employees are people too. They have lives, families, and their own stressors or difficulties within the workday, just like everyone else. If you want your application to stand out from the hundreds of other applications on the desk, the best thing to do is to call your local Social Security case manager and introduce yourself in a kind and friendly manner and offer to help with any aspects of the case in order to make the Social Security worker's life easier and better. This will expedite the processing of your case and the moving of your case from the SSA District Office to the DDS office.

Social Security workers are used to being yelled at and receiving hostile phone calls all day long from people who feel that the case is taking too long to process or by people who feel that the case should be worked in a different manner. Imagine how welcoming your friendly call is to the Social Security worker who is used to being yelled at all day long by other people and other Claimants.

I can promise you, after working on 1000's cases, that your friendly phone call will be received warmly and eagerly by the Social Security Case Manager who is working on your case. Make sure that the worker has all of your contact and application information correct, and get their name and telephone extension number, and fax number. Confirm that all of the forms have been submitted properly.

They will also answer any questions relating to SSI or SSDI. They will answer questions to you relating to onset dates and who is your Disability Determination Services worker (if it has been assigned), and then will answer most any other questions that you may have in regards to your Social Security case.

Remember when you were at school when you were younger, and you were given the advice to bring your teacher an apple to put on the teacher's desk. It's the same approach here.

Just like you used to bring an apple to the teacher to put on their desks so that you would stand out from all your other students and be in the good graces of your teacher, so too by picking up the phone and being friendly and courteous and introducing yourself to your Social Security worker, as well as offering to help by supplying them with whatever missing documentation they need, it's as if you're bringing an apple to the Social Security worker who is working on your claim. They are not going to chase after you, if you are missing a required SSA form. The best thing to do is to again inquire if your application was properly submitted, or if any other form is still outstanding.

You have to remember that there are many forms that must be completed in order for your Social Security application to move forward. If you have an attorney assisting you on the case, you will need to complete the Appointment of Representative form, which is called the SSA-1696.

You will also need to complete the Authorization to Disclose Information to the Social Security Administration form or the SSA-827. If you have an attorney, you will also need to make sure that the SSA District Office has a copy of the Attorney Fee Agreement between you and your attorney, as well as make sure that you timely file any of the appeals that you may have to file in order to move your case forward.

If you want your Social Security worker to look favorably on you and on your case and help you along the way, you must develop a rapport with that worker. And the best way to do that is to call your SSA worker and introduce yourself.

I will note that some District Office have recently tried to stream-line all of the incoming calls at their local District Offices by having their Case Workers answer any questions that you may have when you call in, rather than transfer the call to the specific worker who is working your case. That is fine. As long as you confirm with your local SSA District Office that all forms are in and complete and that the case is being properly processed in a timely fashion, then you are good to go.

After filing you application or appeal, always call the local SSA District Office to confirm that everything was done correctly.

Tip #10: Stay in Touch with the Attorney

THERE IS A LONG PATH from the beginning to the end of the Social Security disability process.

There is a long journey from initial application to approval and then payment.

We must agree and establish that the pathway to success is filled with challenges and hurdles which must be overcome in order to win your case at different times.

There are several partnerships that are part of the Social Security process. And, I am going to mention this concept several times throughout this book.

The first partnership is between you and the Social Security Administration.

The second partnership is between you and Disability Determination Services.

The third partnership is between you and the Social Security Office of Hearings and Operations.

But wait, there is more...

The next partnership is between you and your medical providers, as well as a partnership between you and your attorney.

Finally, the last partnership, which is the most important, is the partnership between you and yourself.

That is when you make a deal with yourself that you're going to do everything you need to do in order to win this case.

But let's focus back on the partnership between you and the attorney.

Yes, the doctors that treat you for your medical conditions are essential to the outcome of your case because of the essential medical notes that they provide to the Social Security Administration. But, in reality, there is no other personality or individual that is more invested in your case besides you than your attorney.

From the first time you get in touch with your attorney and you introduce yourself until the final moments when the attorney says, "Congratulations, you've won your case," your attorney is walking side-by-side with you the entire way.

You must stay in touch with your attorney.

The only way that the attorney knows how to move forward on a case is if you stay in touch with him or her. Often, the attorney needs to fill in forms that must be provided to the Social Security Administration. The attorney needs to call doctors and other medical providers to request medical records on your behalf.

The attorney needs to cultivate and develop arguments for the Judge, as well as submit all the medical records and other documentation into the hearing Exhibit file. The attorney has quite a bit that needs to be done in order to help you win your case.

In my experience in representing thousands of clients, I generally win cases of clients who stay in touch with my office regularly. We speak or trade emails at least every 30 days, if not more.

Don't ever be afraid to call or email your disability attorney for an update on your case.

If your attorney doesn't call you back, then call again. If necessary, leave several messages with the legal assistant or secretary.

Ideally, you want to be able to get your attorney on the telephone and strategize with your attorney on what you need to do to put your application in the best light in order for it to get approved by SSA. This strategizing can only occur if you are regularly in touch with your attorney.

I coach all of my clients from day 1 on what they need to do to win their case. From going to the doctor to how to fill out the SSA forms, I need to be involved. I want to be involved.

Why?

Because I want you to win!

Tip #11: A DMV Handicap Placard is NOT a Disability Determination

I'M OFTEN ASKED BY my disabled clients why the disability eligibility process with the Social Security Administration is so difficult and time-consuming, especially after they've already been awarded a handicap or disability placard from the Department of Motor Vehicles.

We're all aware of what a handicap or disability placard looks like for the Department of Motor Vehicles — it is the figure of the person sitting in a wheelchair that is usually in blue and white. Yes, the blue placard that is hanging from your rear-view mirror or that is painted in the parking spaces designated for handicapped drivers.

Many people innocently asked me if the Department of Motor Vehicles already found me disabled, why do I still need to apply for disability benefits?

The answer is very simple.

The reason a disability application is still needed with the Social Security Administration is that disability determinations made by the Social Security Administration are different than disability determinations made by the Department of Motor Vehicles. Each state has its own Department of Motor Vehicles. And the laws, rules, and disability definitions vary from state to state, and agency to agency.

The legal definition for the federal Social Security Program is *"the inability to engage in any substantial gainful activity (SGA) by reason of any medically determinable physical or mental impairment(s) which can be expected to result in death or which has lasted or can be expected to last for a continuous period of not less than 12 months."*

The disability definition or requirements by your state DMV, on the other hand, can be radically different than the definition of disability by the Social Security Administration. Having said that, the fact that you have a handicap placard from your state DMV is not a 100% guarantee that you will win your disability case with SSA.

Why?

Because the definitions of "disability" are different from agency to agency, and you still need to go through all of the steps and jump over all of the hoops in order to get Social Security Administration to make a finding of disability under <u>their</u> rules.

The same can be said of the Veterans Affairs (VA) definition of "disability." It is not the same definition as the Social Security Administration "disability" definition.

It is important to note that a handicap placard, which has been signed off by your doctor with the DMV, is often very telling and can often make the difference in a disability hearing case before a Judge. It should always be submitted to SSA. Why? Because once the Judge sees that your doctor has signed off on your disability for the DMV, it is considered persuasive evidence.

But, it is not the final say in the matter. The definition of "disabled" at the DMV is always going to be different from the Social Security Administration's definition.

Tip #12: Prescribed Assistive Devices

VERY OFTEN, MY CLIENTS ask me what they can do to improve their chances of winning the case. My answer is always the same - "medical records, medical records, and medical records."

Your entire case and the outcome of your case are based solely on the findings and the objective findings in your medical records.

Whether it be by proper laboratory studies or other testing combinations, your medical records are what will determine the strength of your case and whether or not you get approved for benefits.

What is also helpful and what the Judges and Social Security Administration often look for is if the individual has been prescribed assistive devices, whether it be a back brace, an ankle brace, a knee brace, a hand brace, an elbow brace, a shoulder brace, a neck brace, oxygen, cane, crutches, wheelchair, walker or ambulatory electronic device.

Prescribed assistive devices are very telling as to the severity of your medical impairments.

Often, I'm confronted with a situation where a person uses a brace, cane, or some other assistive device, but that ambulatory assistive device was just purchased from the local drugstore. Perhaps, someone is just using crutches or a brace that they found around the house that was left over from another family member who previously used it. This happens all the time.

Please note that this scenario is not sufficient and carries very little or no weight at all, depending on the Judge.

Since April 2021, when SSA updated their rules and listings, in order for the assistive device to have any weight at all in the outcome of the case, it must be **prescribed** by a medical professional <u>and</u> documented in the medical records. Some Judges don't even accept a prescription by a physician's assistant.

So, if you just go and you use an assistive device that is not prescribed, you will not necessarily win your case because Social Security is now requiring that the doctor prescribe the assistive device and have it clearly stated in the medical record that it is medically necessary.

I will add at this point, even though it is not an assistive device, is the discussion of prescription medical marijuana.

Suffice it to say, for now, that even though Social Security is a federal program, and federal law has not yet approved medical marijuana, if you are prescribed a medical marijuana card from your doctor in your state, the federal Administrative Law Judge will not give you a hard time at the hearing and will accept the prescribed medical marijuana as medically necessary. Your attorney will have to introduce the issue of the medical marijuana card to the Judge, but it won't be a problem in most cases if you are taking it for pain or some other physical medical condition. It can be an issue as it relates to mental impairment, but we will cover that in a later chapter in this book.

Everything must be prescribed by a doctor. Gone are the days when you could just go and purchase an assistive device. Now, everything must be documented and prescribed by your doctor.

Tip #13: Just Answer the Question

ALL DISABILITY HEARINGS before an Administrative Law Judge start the same way.

The Judge will confirm your name, Social Security number, date of birth, and home address.

Simple right?

Ideally, a simple question deserves a simple answer.

Unfortunately, unless the client is prepared by their attorney on how to answer questions, they may not understand that the questions need to be answered simply and directly to the point.

You have to remember that at your hearing, you are going to be given a limited amount of time to present your case to the Judge. Having said that, you want to make your answers short and to the point.

Question, answer.

Question, answer.

It is as simple as that!

Often you will find that human nature is such that when asked a question, a person naturally may answer the question in a run-on sentence or long narrative paragraphs. In some situations, it may be appropriate to give a long narrative paragraph or a run-on answer, but not for the purposes of a court hearing on the record. That is not what the Judge is looking for in your response. The Judge is looking specifically for a short and direct answer to a short and direct question.

Many clients don't realize they often actually get themselves in trouble by providing a long narrative answer.

The reason for this is that there is a tendency for people to talk and talk and talk, and when they talk, they begin to blabber. When they begin to blabber, they begin to lose track of what the original question was. In many cases, they may even provide information that is harmful to their case and which hurts their chances of getting approved.

Don't blabber.

It's very simple — just answer the question!

Tip #14: A Strong Attorney

IT IS ESSENTIAL TO have an attorney who believes in your case.

It is also very crucial to have an attorney who is intelligent and who is able to communicate ideas thoroughly and completely from one person to another. But, not to be overlooked, it is also important to have an attorney who is very 'strong.'

And by 'strong,' I do not mean physically strong.

We are not looking for a bodybuilder.

I mean that your attorney should have a 'strong' character and personality and will not allow themselves to be pushed around in court hearings.

Clearly, even though your disability hearing is considered a "non-adversarial process", the reality is that you are on one side, and the Judge is on the other. You only have one chance in front of the Judge to establish that you are disabled.

In these circumstances and situations, the Judge or the expert witness may try to push the case in a certain direction that is not in your favor. It is at that point that the attorney must be strong and forceful and put a halt to the unfair practice of manipulating a case in order to seek out a specific conclusion.

Characteristics of a 'strong' attorney include, but are not limited to, talking with confidence, talking firmly, talking to the point, and talking with passion.

Passion is a very important criterion for a good attorney. Unless an attorney is passionate about their client's case, they don't stand a chance of winning their claim for benefits.

The most effective attorneys are not only passionate but, as we said above, are also intelligent, have self-confidence, have a strong backbone, and will not let their client get pushed around during the hearing.

One of the most important parts of the hearing is the opening statement that is made by the attorney and which outlines the theory of the case. Your attorney needs to shine and sparkle during this opening statement as it introduces important and essential information to the Judge to consider when reviewing your claim for benefits.

A weak attorney is going to flop on the opening statement and leave out essential aspects of the case which need to be highlighted. A strong attorney has the case under control and speaks with confidence. He or she is "in it to win it." They have a complete grasp of the facts of the case and speak with passion to persuade the Judge to evaluate the evidence and approve the claim.

The best way to gauge your attorney's strength is to read the reviews online.

By reading online review, you will very quickly get a glimpse into the persona and abilities of your respective attorney.

Look for a 5-star rating on Google.

The reviews by former clients are very informative and will navigate you in the right direction to select a 'strong' attorney who you definitely want in your corner.

Tip #15: Having an Experienced Attorney

HAVING AN EXPERIENCED attorney who has hundreds of actual court cases under their belt is a good step in the right direction toward winning your claim for benefits.

The last thing any client wants is to be represented by an inexperienced disability attorney. And it happens more often than you think.

No one wants to lose their case if their attorney is just learning how to present disability cases and is new to the disability industry.

The difference between a good attorney and a great attorney is that a good attorney knows how to present the case. But, a great attorney knows how to win a case.

This only comes from practice and experience.

The best way for an attorney learn his or her way around the courtroom and how to present the case is to have already represented several hundreds of clients before SSA Administrative Law Judges.

Only by having experienced several hundred hearing cases has the attorney seen every scenario possible and is capable of meeting head-on any challenges made to the claim of whether or not a client is disabled or not. Having represented thousands of cases myself, I cannot under-emphasize the importance of having this basic courtroom experience.

1. Do you want to have an attorney who's not familiar with the SSA disability listings and grid rules? (more on that later in this book)
2. Do you want an attorney who's not familiar with how to formulate a theory of the case? (this will also be discussed further in the upcoming topics)
3. Do you want an attorney who is not familiar with how to cross-examine a vocational witness at a hearing before a Judge? (this will also

    be discussed further in the upcoming topics)

4. Do you want an attorney who has never made an opening or closing statement? (yes, this will also be discussed further in the upcoming topics)

The answer is...of course not.

Every person really only has one opportunity before the Judge to present their case in the best light.

Make sure you have an experienced attorney!

Tip #16: Keep Medical Providers in the Loop

OFTEN, MY CLIENTS HAVE come to me saying that their doctor doesn't think that they're disabled.

Yikes!

Alternatively, my clients come to me and state that the doctor refuses to fill out a Residual Functional Capacity (RFC) questionnaire that helps establish a client's exertional limitations. A Residual Functional Capacity questionnaire is a short list of questions that outline your restrictions and limitations in the opinion of your treating physician.

I'm always bewildered by my clients who continue to visit medical providers who are not interested in being involved in the disability process.

In order to make your case easier to get approved, your medical provider should know all the details of your medical condition(s), as well as your physical limitations or mental limitations. He or she should have the old, as well as the new, information regarding your medical health and limitations clearly noted in the medical record.

Your medical provider must be involved in the process because they need to understand that the medical notes must be well documented. The medical records will be requested and reviewed by the Judge, and the notes they put in the records WILL make all the difference in the final outcome.

Suppose your doctor writes in the medical records generic language that *"the patient is stable"* or that *"the medical findings and examination were within normal limits."* Before you even know what is happening, the case will be denied.

*Let's be clear. I am **NOT** saying that your medical providers should be fabricating or making up medical notes to help you get approved. That is fraud!*

What I am saying is that your medical provider should be aware of the fact that you applied for disability benefits, so that they can support you in your claim for benefits.

Their awareness of your claim for benefits will be reflected by their willingness to assist you in the process by either completing the Residual Functional Capacity questionnaire or by making sure that they properly notate everything in the medical records.

If your doctor does not want to be a partner in this process, then you should find another doctor. You are going to need your doctors help to get approved.

You need to remember that the medical provider is one of the key partners in this process which we keep emphasizing throughout this book over and over again. And there is a good reason for it!

Your medical provider must be on your team and must play a role in helping you to win your case!

Tip #17: Telephone Shortcuts

ONE OF THE BIGGEST issues that my clients have are the long wait times they encounter when calling the Social Security Administration.

First of all, don't ever call the national SSA number, unless you want to be on hold for 45-60 minutes.

You are better off checking with www.ssa.gov, if all you need is status on your claim for benefits.

But, if you actually need to speak to an SSA Representative, you always want to call your <u>local</u> SSA District Office.

The difference in waiting time is easily 45-60 minutes when you call the national SSA hotline, versus an 8-12 minutes wait time when you call your local SSA District Office.

Here is a shortcut when calling your local SSA District office.

As soon as the Social Security Welcome message comes on at the local District Office and the telephone system allows you to enter a prompt, you should push one for English (or 2 for Spanish, if that is your preferred language). As the voice begins to speak according to the language chosen, you will be given a menu of choices to make a choice from.

Once the next prompt ends, you should push **TWO to continue with your call and then ZERO** for the next field office operator.

By following this technique with the local SSA District Office telephone number, you will no longer have to wait for them for 45 minutes, but a much more reasonable 8-12 minutes.

I wish I had known this tip of NOT calling the National SSA number years ago.

I could have saved myself so much wasted time waiting for the national representative to pick up the phone.

Now, I just call the local SSA District Offices and use the telephone shortcuts above instead of listening to the long-recorded telephone prompts.

You will find that your local District Office will not only be quicker to get on the phone, but will also be able to provide you with more updated information on your claim.

It is important to also note that each SSA District Office has a fax number. Get that fax number! Write it down! Use it!

If you have anything that needs to be submitted in to SSA to review, make sure that you either hand-deliver it to your local SSA office, mail it in or fax it in. Make sure you keep the fax receipt.

Communication is an essential part of success. If you want to be successful in winning your disability claim, you need to be able to communicate, specifically with SSA.

If someone needs to wait 45-60 minutes each time they call SSA, they will surely lose their mind.

Try calling your local SSA District office instead of the national SSA hotline, and you will find that it is not as hard as you may have previously experienced to get in touch with and communicate with SSA.

Tip #18: Never Interrupt the Judge

WHEN YOU'RE IN A COURTROOM, you are at the mercy of the court and the Judge.

Remember, the Judge is the King or Queen, and you are in their little kingdom.

You want the court and the Judge to look at your case favorably and approve your case.

You want the court and Judge to have everything they need so the case goes smoothly during your trial.

The last thing you want to do is upset the Judge during the hearing.

Would you be surprised if I told you that the easiest way to upset the Judge is to simply interrupt the Judge every time he or she tries to speak? That's right. Never interrupt the Judge.

Otherwise, things for you are just going to go from bad to worse.

It goes without saying that you also need to be respectful to the Judge. Only refer to the Judge as "Sir," "Ma'am" or "Your Honor." I think that's pretty self-explanatory.

Judges are very quick to lose their patience, and their demeanor will switch when they feel that they're being rudely interrupted or cut off mid-sentence.

So, whatever you do, no matter what... NEVER interrupt the Judge.

Tip #19: SSI Gets Medicaid, and SSDI Gets Medicare

———

IF YOU APPROVED FOR Social Security Disability benefits, you are entitled to a disability benefits package.

As discussed, the Social Security Administration offers two different types of disability programs.

The first program is called **Supplemental Security Income (SSI)**, which is a need-based program. Eligibility to this program not only takes into consideration your medical condition, but also your residency, resources, income, and citizenship.

The second program is **Social Security Disability Insurance (SSDI)**, where eligibility is based on the number of active work credits you have earned throughout your career.

In general, the Social Security has a benefit calculation they use based on your averaged earnings which will determine how much money you get if you are awarded disability benefits.

The amount of money you get for SSI benefits depends on the state that you live in and the state amount, which is a flat amount for every SSI recipient. In addition to the cash benefits that are awarded, many people don't realize there is also an additional benefit, which to some people may even be even more important than the cash benefits. That benefit is the award of health insurance.

Once you've been approved for SSI, then together with your cash award, in most states, you will also receive Medicaid health benefits, which start the first month after your award date. This means that not only will you get money, but exactly one month from your award date, Medicaid will kick in and will allow you easy access to Medicaid doctors, hospitals, and other essential services.

SSDI, on the other hand, allows the beneficiary to opt-in to additional Medicare benefits together with the cash benefits.

The Medicare benefits, which are a part of the SSDI program, kick in 29 months after the *onset date* or 24 months after the *entitlement date*.

What is the difference between the *'onset date'* and the *'entitlement date?'*

The *onset date* is the date on the calendar when Social Security determines that you are medically disabled.

Your *entitlement date* is after you have been found medically disabled for the SSDI program <u>and</u> you have completed the required five-month eligibility waiting period to receive your benefits.

As such, you get Medicare 24 months from the entitlement date.

The five-month waiting period is often frowned upon by many disability beneficiaries since they want their complete benefits package right away. Unfortunately, the way the law is written is that each person must wait five complete months from their onset date before they're entitled to either cash benefits or their Medicare benefits. As mentioned above, many people are just as interested or more interested in the health care benefits as they are in the cash benefits.

The reason for that is simple…many people have barriers to accessing quality health care, so by being awarded health benefits like Medicaid or Medicare, a person can access quality medical services and providers and obtain the treatment they need.

In Which States Does Social Security Automatically Enroll SSI Recipients in Medicaid?

THE DISTRICT OF COLUMBIA and the following thirty-four states let Social Security determine Medicaid eligibility using SSI criteria. They also allow Social Security to automatically enroll SSI recipients in Medicaid.

Alabama, Arizona, Arkansas, California, Colorado, Delaware, Florida, Georgia, Indiana, Iowa, Kentucky, Louisiana, Maine, Maryland, Massachusetts, Michigan, Mississippi, Montana, New Jersey, New Mexico, New York, North Carolina, Ohio, Pennsylvania, Rhode Island, South Carolina, South Dakota, Tennessee, Texas, Vermont, Washington, West Virginia, Wisconsin, and Wyoming.

Which States Require a Separate Medicaid Application but Guarantee Eligibility for SSI Recipients?

A FEW STATES MAKE THEIR own Medicaid eligibility decisions using the same income, resource, and disability criteria that Social Security uses for the SSI program. Alaska, Idaho, Kansas, Nebraska, Nevada, Oregon, Utah, and the Northern Mariana Islands all make their own Medicaid eligibility decisions using SSI criteria. That means that everyone who receives SSI in those jurisdictions should qualify for Medicaid. These states, however, require you to file a separate Medicaid application. Which States Don't Guarantee Medicaid Eligibility for SSI Recipients?

Nine states have decided to use eligibility criteria for Medicaid that are more restrictive than the SSI program. In most of those states, SSI recipients will find that the rules about income and resources or the definition of disability are stricter for Medicaid than they are for SSI. Luckily, the federal government has imposed rules to limit how restrictive the states can be when screening SSI recipients for Medicaid eligibility.

States with Their Own Medicaid Eligibility Criteria

THE NINE STATES ARE Connecticut, Hawaii, Illinois, Minnesota, Missouri, New Hampshire, North Dakota, Oklahoma, and Virginia.

So, there you have it....

Congratulations on winning your Social Security Disability case!

Not only will you get your cash benefits, but in most cases, you will also get either Medicaid or Medicare benefits as well.

Tip #20: Your SSDI Award

WHEN YOU WIN YOUR SSI case, your award is usually a flat dollar amount award from the state, and generally every SSI beneficiary in the state receives the same dollar amount.

The 2023 SSI Federal Benefit Rate (FBR) for an individual living in his or her own household and with no other countable income is **$914 monthly**; the SSI benefit rate for a couple (with both husband and wife eligible) is $1,371 monthly. Check online to see what the SSI award is for your state.

With SSDI, on the other hand, the award is based on *how much you paid into the system over the course of your career.*

During each paycheck, while you were employed, you made a payment to the Social Security Administration. This payment is not only for your retirement benefits, but it is also for disability benefits in the event that you become disabled. The amount of money that you pay into the system will determine what your award will be if you are found disabled.

For instance, if you worked in Walmart and earned $12 an hour, the amount you paid into the SSA program each payroll period would be substantially different than if you were someone who had another type of job that earned a much larger income over the course of their career. Because the amount that you paid into the SSA program would be substantially greater than that of an employee at Walmart, you will get a greater benefit amount once awarded disability benefits.

In 2023, the data tells us that the average monthly benefit amount paid to an SSDI recipient is **around $1,358,** but can go as high as around **$3,627** a month for those whose income was fairly high in recent years.

Your benefits amount is called your **Primary Insurance Amount (PIA)**, and is calculated as follows:

- 90% of the first slice (your first $1,115 from your Average Indexed Monthly Earnings or AIME), PLUS

- 32% of the second slice (any AIME between $1,116 and $6,721), PLUS

- 15% of the third portion (any AIME over $6,721)

Remember, the amount you receive each month will be based on the average lifetime earnings you made before your disability began. This is the only factor that determines your benefit amount. In other words, your SSDI benefit amount isn't based on how severe your disability is or even your age; it is based, using the calculation above, on how much you earned over the course of your career.

If you had to collect SSDI, do you know what your SSDI Primary Insurance Amount benefit amount is?

You can easily check it by calling your local SSA District Office or logging into your www.ssa.gov[1] page for the most updated information.

You generally must have at least 40 active work credits as an adult in order to qualify for SSDI benefits.

---

1. http://www.ssa.gov

Tip #21: Turn Your Case Around

OVER THE COURSE OF my career, I've met many clients who have come to me midway through the process of applying for disability benefits.

They often come to me because they were referred after either getting discouraged by trying to win the benefits on their own or having a bad experience with another attorney.

They come to me depressed and downtrodden and unsure of how they're going to win their case.

They're convinced that they will lose their case even though the Social Security Administration hasn't made a final decision.

I have to reassure them from the start that until a decision is made, there is still time to turn their case around.

What do I mean by *turning your case around?*

Well, the first thing is that until a decision is made by a Judge, you can still submit any evidence you want to the Social Security Administration for them to consider as part of your application process. This means there is still time for you to submit new medical records, new laboratory findings, new X-rays, new MRI results, or any other documentation that you feel will support your case.

So, until that decision is made by the Judge, you have plenty of time to submit whatever you want. New medical records, new surgical notes, DMV disability placards, mental health therapy notes, updated medical lists, and testimonial letters from old employers or family members. In the event that a decision has been made and you were denied, all hope is not lost since there several appeal levels associated with a Social Security application.

All cases begin with the initial application, which hopefully is approved.

If it is not approved and it is denied, what can be done in this situation?

Commonly, you can make a request for Reconsideration of the denied application. What that means is that the application is sent back to the Disability Determination Services, DDS, for another look at the case by a fresh set of eyes.

During the Reconsideration appeal, you can again submit any information you want or any documentation you want for the Social Security Administration to consider

Hopefully, your request for Reconsideration will be approved. Unfortunately, there's about a 15% reversal rate nationally. That means you have an 85% chance of losing the Reconsideration level, and you probably will have to file a request for a hearing before an Administrative Law Judge.

The wait time for a hearing before an Administrative Law Judge is anywhere from 6 to 12 months, depending on the state where you live. It used to be 18 to 24 months, but Social Security has done a great job of eliminating the backlog and speeding up the process. Now, depending on what state you're in, you will have to wait between 6-12 months for a hearing date before the Administrative Law Judge.

In different chapters of this book, we will discuss the process of what a hearing is like. But for now, let's focus on how the case can be turned around in your favor. During the hearing, you will present all the evidence that you want for the Judge to consider approving your case.

Once the Judge decides and issues the decision, it is either going to be favorable, partially favorable, or unfavorable.

If it is a favorable decision, congratulations, you have won your case.

A partially favorable decision means that your case was approved, but perhaps with a different *onset date* than you originally applied with or for a closed period of benefits, meaning that the Judge did not grant your ongoing benefits. If it's a partially favorable or unfavorable decision, then you can again appeal this decision to the Social Security Administration Appeals Council.

There is about a 5% reversal rate nationally on Appeals Council cases. You may be one of the lucky ones who gets the case reversed and/or remanded for another hearing or even to get approved.

But in most cases, you will end up in federal court if the SSA Appeals Council affirms the original Judge's decision.

Finally, it is important to note that the most important and easiest way to turn your case around is to retain an attorney to assist you in the eligibility and/or appeals process – especially if you haven't had your hearing yet. You will substantially increase your odds of winning your case anytime you have an attorney representing you.

I think what you need to take away from this chapter is that you have many chances and ways to turn your case around and get approved. Just because you were denied at one level, never give up!

KEEP APPEALING!

GET AN ATTORNEY!

SUBMIT YOUR NEW MEDICAL RECORDS!

NEVER GIVE UP!

TURN YOUR CASE AROUND!

Tip #22: Medical Records, Medical Records, Medical Records!

I'VE SAID IT BEFORE, and I'll say it again. You cannot win your case unless you have medical records which support your claim for disability, which are well documented and which have no gaps in the treatment dates.

The key to success, in any case, is having medical records, medical records, medical records!

Over the years, I've often represented Claimants who told me when I accepted the case that they were regularly seeing their doctor, only for me to discover days before the hearing that there were, in fact, very few medical records.

When I would pick up the phone to call these Claimants and ask them where all of their medical records were, they would reply that they didn't have time to go see the doctor or that they had no insurance.

Steam would blow out of my ears out of frustration and aggravation that a Claimant would take a year and a half to wait for a hearing, and not make the most of the waiting time by regularly visiting the doctor or even an emergency room if they need medical attention. The only way the Social Security Administration or a Judge can approve your case is if you have medical records!

What can be more important than going to the doctor? First and foremost, if you're not going to the doctor to help your case, you should at least be going to the doctor for your own health. Who wants to be in pain? Why live a life where you can't enjoy your friends and family? What about your medications?

People should also be going to the doctor to make sure they live a long, healthy, and productive life. The theory of procrastination is the other reason why people don't go to the doctor at all. Often, they are afraid or fearful that the doctor will give them bad news about their health. Unfortunately, we cannot run away from reality, and we must face our doctors and face the circumstances which are presented before us.

You should go to the doctor routinely to check if there aren't any issues or problems with your health — whether it be issues with the musculoskeletal system, respiratory system, cardiovascular system, or any other part of your body. If you regularly visit the doctor, you will know before something gets really bad so that it can be treated in a timely fashion. This is why it is essential that you go see your doctor and try to maintain good health.

How are you supposed to be prescribed medication if you don't go to the doctor? Each medical ailment requires a certain medication to treat that medical condition, so if you don't go to the doctor, you cannot be prescribed medication.

One of the main things that a Judge looks for in a case is what medications have been prescribed to you. Mental and emotional health also requires the regular oversight of a doctor. You cannot expect to win a case for depression, common anxiety, schizophrenia, or post-traumatic stress disorder unless you regularly go see a mental health specialist.

Ideally, you should be visiting a therapist or a psychologist at least once a month, if not once a week, for an entire year in order to develop your mental claim for benefits. In addition to seeing a psychologist or therapist, you need to see a psychiatrist who will prescribe you medication. Some people cannot afford a psychologist or psychiatrist, so they allow their primary care physician (PCP) just to prescribe the medication. This should only be done as a last resort.

Ideally, a person should find a separate psychologist and psychiatrist to treat them for their mental and emotional health. Do not expect to win your case unless you're getting regular treatment from a doctor. I can't emphasize that enough. The PCP is not enough, even though he/she is prescribing you medication.

As we have mentioned in an earlier chapter, it's also important to realize that your doctor has to be your partner in the disability process. Your doctor must believe in your case and hopefully help you by writing a letter regarding the severity of your condition to the Social Security Administration.

Unless your doctor is willing to assist you in the process and be a partner in this journey, you may not win your case. If your doctor is not willing to assist in this process, you should discuss the reason behind their decision not to help you with them. If necessary, you should also go ahead and find another doctor who will be your partner. You cannot win unless you have a doctor as your partner.

Make sure you call your doctor to keep your medical records and medications updated. Your medical records and an experienced disability attorney are the 2 most important pieces needed to win your claim for benefits!

Tip #23: You Attorney is Your Partner

AS PREVIOUSLY DISCUSSED, there are many partners and many players in the Social Security process.

One of the partners is your doctor, and the other partner is your attorney, who represents you and is looking out for your best interests during the case. Many people hire attorneys because they are unclear of the process or unclear about the rules that Social Security looks for when reviewing a case.

Hopefully, you've made a wise choice in selecting an attorney who is familiar with all the disability rules and regulations.

Your attorney will assist you from day one with a proper screening so that he/she can evaluate the strength of your case. Your attorney will help you with all the paperwork that needs to be completed in a timely fashion. During the application process, your attorney should follow up with you to help you complete the Social Security Administration Function Report, the Work History report, and any other forms that are sent to you to be completed by the Social Security Administration.

Your attorney will act as a liaison between you and the Social Security Administration. He or she will contact the local District Office as needed in order to make sure that the case is being processed correctly and on time. Your attorney will also act as a liaison between you and the Department of Disability Determination Services, DDS, to make sure that they are properly requesting all the medical records and that all the medical records are being submitted.

It is important to note that if your case is denied at the application level, your attorney will assist you with completing all of the forms necessary for a Request for Reconsideration. Not only will the attorney complete the appeal forms for the Request for Reconsideration, but he or she will also help prepare the disability report appeal form. That is also a requirement when filing an appeal.

The attorney will act as your partner to make sure that DDS is requesting all the medical records timely and proper. And that everything is being submitted to the record. Your attorney's responsibility is to call the DDS worker regularly and frequently to get the status of your case and provide any missing information. In the event that the Reconsideration isn't approved, your attorney should also help prepare the forms for a Request for Hearing before an Administrative Law Judge.

As you prepare for your hearing before an Administrative Law Judge, I cannot emphasize enough the attorney's role in helping make sure that you have all the documents and medical records necessary to win your case. Remember that the medical records submitted to the Judge must be in electronic format. The attorney's job is to request all the necessary records and ensure they are submitted in a timely fashion. This will make it easier for the Judge to review them.

Your attorney should also provide you with Residual Functional Capacity (RFC) questionnaires so that your doctor can complete these forms and certify that you are disabled. There are many types of residual functional capacity questionnaires. Some are for physical conditions, and some are for mental conditions. Some have specific forms that are customized to your particular medical condition, while others are general forms that will allow your doctor to certify that you are disabled and/or list out your limitations.

Your attorney should help you prepare all these forms and present them to the Judge. Additionally, your attorney will help you prepare for your hearing before the Administrative Law Judge. Ideally, your attorney should spend 45 to 60 minutes with you explaining the process and going over the Question and Answer format so that you are totally prepared for the style of the hearing and that nothing is a surprise to you on the actual day of the hearing.

Your attorney should also explain to you the role of the Medical Experts and the Vocational Experts at the hearing. The goal is for you to understand what is occurring at the hearing when the Judge is questioning the Medical Expert or the vocational expert. I cannot emphasize enough the importance of having a good attorney and the role that the attorney plays in the success of your case.

A good attorney's office should increase your chances of winning to 70% or 75%, or even 80%.

Make sure you hire a good attorney to help you with your case.

Tip #24: Failure to Comply

WHEN THE JUDGE REVIEWS your medical records, they aren't just looking at the medical records to make sure that you see a doctor frequently and regularly. They are also looking at the notes that the doctor writes down in the medical records. One of the biggest red flags for a Judge and one of the reasons that a Judge denies a claim is when the doctor states *"failure to comply"* with prescribed medication regimens or suggested therapy.

What is the point of having medications prescribed to you if you aren't going to take the medications? The Judge will hold it against you for your failure to take the prescribed medication on time. If you're prescribed medications, you must fill your prescription regularly. And you must take your medication as prescribed by the doctor.

The same goes for physical therapy or occupational therapy, or any other type of therapy sessions that are prescribed to you by the doctor. If a doctor writes the medical notes that you've been prescribed certain therapy or treatments, the Judges will expect you to have those treatments before them. You must play a role in helping yourself out in order to feel better. You cannot expect to ever get approved on a case if you're not listening to your doctor. If your doctors prescribe you medication, you must take the medication.

Sometimes you have a good reason for not taking your medication or going to therapy. Maybe you had no money to purchase medication or pay for therapy. In this case, Judges are sympathetic to this excuse and will overlook the fact that you failed to comply with the medication regimens. In short, you need to provide a good cause explanation for why you didn't comply with the medication regimens or other prescribed courses of action by your doctors.

It is worthwhile to mention, that if DDS or the Judge see that you repeatedly "failed" to attend your scheduled appointments, this can also be a red flag.

Diabetic patients are expected to take all of their insulin and be prescribed diabetic medication.

Heart patients are expected to take all the prescribed heart medication.

Mental health patients are expected to take all the prescribed mental health medication.

You must take the medication prescribed to you by the doctor if you want to win your case.

You will not be punished for deciding to not have a delicate or risky surgery. But your case may blow up in your face, if you fail to comply with the prescribed medication regimen. You never want the doctor to write in your medical records that you failed to comply with their instructions. That's a big no-no!

Tip #25: Auxiliary Children's Benefits

DID YOU KNOW THAT IF you win your Social Security Disability Insurance (SSDI) case, then not only will you receive benefits, but all of your unmarried children under the age of 18 will also receive the same benefits?

That's right!

All of your unmarried children under 18 will receive auxiliary benefits because you won your Social Security Disability Insurance case.

To receive benefits, the child must:

- Be unmarried.

- Be under the age of 18; **or**

- Be 18-19 years old and a full-time student (no higher than grade 12); **or**

- Be 18 or older and disabled from a disability that started before age 22.[1]

Normally, these Auxiliary benefits stop when children reach age 18 unless they are disabled. However, if the child is still a full-time student at a secondary (or elementary) school at age 18, benefits will continue until the child graduates or two months after the child becomes age 19, whichever is first. You should also just be aware that there is a family maximum based on how much you paid into the system.

---

1. https://www.ssa.gov/benefits/disability/qualify.html

During your career, Social Security will calculate your benefits based on how many children you have, how much your benefits are, how much each child is expected to receive. As long as your children meet the criteria outlined above, they will receive auxiliary benefits. It will generally be about 50% of your benefit amount per month, up to the family maximum.

This is another reason to make sure that you get your case approved. Not only will you get your cash benefits and Medicare benefits, but your children will receive auxiliary benefits as a direct deposit right into your bank account. If you're not doing it for yourself, at least do it for your children.

The rationale behind the award of these Auxiliary Benefits is simply that since you, as an adult, are disabled and cannot work, the Social Security Administration is providing additional funding for your children. SSA wants you to be able to purchase food, provide shelter, and purchase clothing, and other essential items for your child's well-being.

Auxiliary benefits should not be overlooked and are an important part of the Social Security process.

If you win your case, after you've been awarded your Social Security Disability Insurance, you should call your local SSA District Office to make sure that they have the names and dates of birth of all your children under the age of 18. This way, all of your children can receive the calculated benefit amounts up until the family maximum has been reached.

Additionally, these benefits can be retroactive all the back to your entitlement date.

Don't forget, if you're not doing it for yourself, then at least do it for your children.

Tip #26: Be on Top of your Medical Records

AT THE BEGINNING OF your application process, the Social Security Administration will ask you for the name, address, and telephone numbers of all your medical providers — whether a hospital, a primary care physician, a clinic, or a specialist you visit. You will have to provide Social Security with all the information so that they can timely request the medical records.

Often clients call me and ask, *"Why is the application process taking so long?"*

The answer is that your medical doctors and providers may not have timely responded to the medical requests for records made by the Social Security Administration.

You must be a partner in your own case, and you must be an advocate for yourself.

Even though the attorney has requested the medical records and is working with you, he or she does not have a relationship with your medical provider(s). Therefore, it is in your best interest to pick up the phone and call your medical providers and alert them to the fact that your medical records are being requested.

Alternatively, you may need to login to your patient portal and download the records yourself. Thereafter, you can submit them yourself to DDS or forward them to your attorney to submit on your behalf.

Let them know that you expect that they will respond to that medical request in a timely fashion. It isn't enough to just send the notes of your psychiatrist to the Social Security Administration. If you see a psychologist or a therapist, you must alert your doctor that they need to also send in the session notes and the detailed notes from the time you spent together in therapy.

I know of many mental health cases that were lost simply because the therapist did not provide the session notes to the Social Security Administration. Be alert! When you visit your doctor, your doctor should be transcribing and writing down all of your medical symptoms and diagnosis. Sometimes we go to the doctor and explain in detail what *we* think is wrong with us based on symptoms or pain. The doctor just listens but doesn't write. Make sure they write it all down!

You should regularly remind your doctor that you are applying for Social Security disability benefits and that it is very important for your doctor to document all of your medical conditions, diagnosis, and symptoms in the medical records. This is especially true for depression, anxiety, schizophrenia, and post-traumatic stress disorder cases.

Unless the Social Security Administration and the Administrative Law Judge can clearly see your therapist session notes, your symptoms, and the severity of your medical conditions, you will lose your case when it comes to mental health cases.

Tip #27: Check Case Status Online

THERE ARE SEVERAL WAYS to check the status of your case.

1. Call the local SSA District Office and speak to them to get a status on your case;
2. Speak to the Disability Determination Service case analyst who has been assigned your case and is working to collect all the medical records.

But, I have found that the best way to check the status of your case in real-time is to go online to www.ssa.gov[1]. The first time you go to www.ssa.gov, you will need to register yourself and have an account with the website.

Once you go ahead and do a first-time registration, you are then able to go to the website at any time of day and on any day of the week, making it easy and convenient to check the status of your case. The website may not give you specifics of the case, but at least it will tell you if the case is pending, approved, or denied.

Once you have that information, you can then call your SSA District Office to make sure that they have everything they need to go ahead and process your case in a timely manner. You can also check your benefit amount online to see *how much* you would be eligible for if you are found disabled. This is called the Primary Insurance Amount or "PIA."

The PIA calculation can be confusing. It is:

- 90% of the first $1,115 of his/her average indexed monthly earnings, plus

- 32% of his/her average indexed monthly earnings over $1,115 and through $6,721, plus

---

1. http://www.ssa.gov

- 15% of his/her average indexed monthly earnings over $6,721.

The Primary Insurance Amount is based on total earnings made over your working career and how much you paid into the system. This is the actual dollar amount you'll receive if you're found disabled and is not the number of credits that you have. Remember, you need 40 active work credits in order to apply for Social Security Disability Insurance.

Once you have accumulated the 40 active work credits, you're able to apply for SSDI.

It is very helpful to you and will give you peace of mind to know that you can always check the status of your case and your PIA amount online at www.ssa.gov[2] .

---

2. http://www.ssa.gov

Tip #28: Cross-Examining the Medical and Vocational Experts

———

CHANCES ARE GOOD THAT there will either be a Medical Expert and/or a Vocational Expert at your hearing.

The Medical Expert will attend the hearing to provide expert testimony to the Judge and to assist the Judge in determining if you meet a Social Security Adult Listing.

The Medical Expert will provide information to the Judge regarding the severity of your medical conditions and will go so far as to tell the Judge in his or her medical expertise if they believe that you're disabled or not and whether you meet the SSA Adult disability listings.

A Vocational Expert, on the other hand, is someone who specializes in employment and job numbers in the national economy. The Vocational Expert has 2 roles at the hearing: (1) to provide testimony to the Judge if a hypothetical individual with the same, age, education and functional capacity as you can return to any of the jobs you have held over the last 15 years and (2) to find if there are any other jobs available in the national economy which can be performed.

The Vocational Expert will first provide detailed information on your past relevant work history for the last 15 years.

They will explain to the Judge whether your job was a sedentary job, a light job, a medium-level job, or a heavy exertional level job, and if past relevant work can be performed. From there, the Judge will go ahead and ask certain hypothetical questions to the Vocational Expert based on your residual functional capacity, and we'll ask the Vocational Experts if they believe that there are other jobs that can be performed under these hypotheticals.

I can guarantee you that the Vocational Expert will easily find at least three jobs that he or she thinks can be performed, no matter how silly those jobs are.

Some of those jobs include:

- Pencil sorter
- Call-Out Operator
- Surveillance System Monitor
- Addressor
- Tube operator, etc.

These are just examples.

The issue for the Judge is not just whether or not you can return to your old job, but also whether or not there are other jobs that a hypothetical person with the same age, education and residual functional capacity as you can perform in the national economy.

In general, if the Vocational Expert can find three jobs which can be performed, chances are that you will lose your case. Your attorney (or you, if you're representing yourself (which I do not recommend)) must cross-examine the Medical Expert and the Vocational Expert. Cross-examining these experts is an art and comes with years of courtroom experience. So, it is not recommended that you go to a hearing without an attorney. In most cases, only an attorney is skilled at cross-examining the Medical Expert and the Vocational Expert.

There are specific questions that the attorney knows how to ask that will help your case and which will erode the number of jobs that are available in the national economy. Don't try to cross-examine the Medical or Vocational Expert on your own, as this will most likely backfire and result in you losing your case. It is highly recommended that you retain a skilled attorney who has had several hundred cases under their belt throughout their career to represent you at the hearing before the Administrative Law Judge.

Remember, the Judge does not have to listen to the expert opinion of the Medical Expert or the Vocational Expert, but their testimony is highly persuasive. So, make sure you have a good attorney who cross-examines them at your hearing.

I always say: <u>**NEVER**</u> **END YOUR HEARING UNTIL YOU GET THE VOCATIONAL EXPERT DOWN TO ZERO JOBS!**

Tip #29: The Dire Needs Letter

THERE ISN'T A DAY THAT goes go by when I don't receive a call from a client who tells me that they are totally out of money and that they are under extreme financial pressure from all sides.

They can't pay for their rent or mortgage, food or medical treatment.

They simply don't know what to do.

They are aware that the average processing time for a disability application can be 6 to 8 months, and they are aware that a reconsideration appeal can be another 6 to 8 months. Unfortunately, if the request for reconsideration is denied, it can be another 8 to 10 months for a hearing date before the Judge.

What can they do?

There is something called a "Dire Needs" request.

A Dire Needs request means that the Claimant is in a "dire situation" and needs an expedited resolution to their claim for benefits.

Unfortunately, Dire Needs cases are very difficult to get approved, and as far as I've seen through my experience in working with thousands and thousands of cases, the only way a Dire Needs request is approved is IF you can show by evidence one of the following:

⬦ You are without food and unable to obtain it;

⬦ You lack medicine or medical care and are unable to obtain it, or access to necessary medical care is restricted because of a lack of resources.

◈ You lack shelter (e.g., without utilities such that their home is uninhabitable, homelessness, expiration of a shelter stay, or imminent eviction or foreclosure with no means to remedy the situation or obtain shelter).

Yes, the criteria and bar are very high for getting approved for a Dire Needs request.

Here is what you need to do if you find yourself in the situation and need an expedited resolution to your disability claim.

If your case is at the Application or Reconsideration level, you must send your Dire Needs request to your local District office.

If your case is pending a hearing date, you must send the Dire Needs request directly to the Judge.

Here is what you need to include with Dire Needs request.

You need to show the Judge or the SSA District Office that you fall into one of the 3 categories listed above.

The best way to prove that is to either attach an eviction notice, a letter from your mortgage company, or a letter from the sheriff showing that you have a date for a *lockout* and send it to your SSA District Office or the Judge, along with a cover sheet, explaining the circumstances and the urgency of your request.

In almost all cases, if you are at risk of being evicted, having your home foreclosed on, or becoming homeless, your Dire Needs request will be approved.

Remember, it is not enough to just send in the request. You need to follow up on it 2 to 3 days after you've faxed it in with the attached documentation to either the District Office or the Judge.

It breaks my heart to know that so many of you are having financial pressure.

I understand that you no longer know how you're going to pay your next bill.

It breaks my heart that many of you can't pay for medication or medical treatment. It breaks my heart to just know that you're anxious and falling apart when you think about your financial situation. I wish the Social Security Administration was more sympathetic.

Your other option is to contact your local Senator or Congress Representative and ask them to call the SSA District Office to have the case expedited. This doesn't always work, but it is worth a shot.

Some SSA District Offices and hearing offices are very responsive when they get a call from a Senator or representative from Congress, and others are not because they have to abide by the regulations which state that the person must be at risk of becoming homeless.

As such, if you fall into one of the 3 categories listed above, my tip to you is to submit a Dire Needs request as soon as possible.

Hopefully, that will do the trick to get you bumped up in the line.

Tip #30: Step Three Approval

IT ISN'T JUST ABOUT meeting the non-medical requirements for disability eligibility, but you must also meet the medical requirements.

When deciding whether or not to approve your case for benefits, SSA follows a 5-Step Sequential Evaluation for determining medical disability.

These 5 steps are:

1. Is the individual engaging in Substantial Gainful Activity (SGA)? Those who make over $1,470/month in 2023 in countable income are considered engaging in SGA and do not qualify for disability benefits.

2. Is the individual's physical and/or mental condition severe? A person whose condition is a) severe enough to prevent work and b) is expected to last longer than 12 months or result in death is considered to have a severe impairment.

3. Does the individual's medical condition meet or equal the severity of a listing? To determine this, SSA compares an applicant's diagnosis to that condition's listing in the Social Security Disability, which you can find at any time online. The best way to review the SSA Adult Listings is to either visit www.ssa.gov[1] or Google "SSA Adult Listings" for a complete list.

4. Can an individual do any of his/her past relevant work? Those who show an inability to function well enough or are safe enough to return to any of their past jobs in the last 15 years.

---

1. http://www.ssa.gov

5. Can the individual make an adjustment to any other work? If a person's condition, age, education, and work experience are found to disqualify them from any other work, they are found to be disabled.

In order to win your case, you generally will always need to complete the 5-step sequential evaluation successfully. The Judge will meticulously perform the 5-Step sequential evaluation and will outline his or her findings in the decision after the hearing.

The ideal strategy to winning the case in your favor, however, is to be found disabled at Step 3.

Why at step #3? Because if you meet steps 1, 2 and 3, you automatically win, without the need to go to steps 4 and 5.

You are a "Winner-Winner-Chicken Dinner!"

I know many of you are lost. So, let's use a visualization tool:

The best way to understand Step 3 is to visualize that a bunch of SSA doctors all came together in a room and voted in agreement that in order to be found medically *disabled*, you need your medical records to show specific pieces of medical evidence. Those are the Adult Disability Listings. Each medical condition was broken down into specific *listings*, and each *listing* represents another body part of a medical condition.

A Step 3 finding means that all of your medical records exactly match up or equal one the SSA Adult listings. These listings can be found online by googling "SSA Adult Listings." Check it out by selecting your medical condition from a list of medical conditions and see if your medical condition meets a Social Security Disability Listing.

(Note: I originally included all of the Disability listings in this book, but it added an extra 375 pages, so I opted to remove them and just navigate you online so that we could keep the book concise and easy to read ☺).

The key to winning the case at Step #3 is to make sure __all__ your medical records are assembled and ready to be presented to the Judge in their entirety.

I cannot emphasize enough the importance of gathering all your updated medical records.

The only way to win a Step #3 approval is to have very supportive medical records, with no treatment gaps, that document the medical condition, as well as a completed Residual Functional Capacity (RFC) questionnaire, which is completed by your primary care physician and/or mental health provider.

This will help you win at Step #3, so that you can avoid going to Steps 4 and 5 of the sequential evaluation. As a strategy, always try with your attorney to get Step 3 approval when before the Judge.

Tip #31: The Five Steps to Win

THE SOCIAL SECURITY Administration (SSA) uses a Five-Step Sequential Evaluation when considering an adult's application for disability benefits.

SSA is always required to go through this process when deciding whether to award or deny an application for benefits.

If you want to truly understand the step-by-step process of how SSA decides whether or not to approve or deny your case, here it is:

Step 1: Are you engaged in Substantial Gainful Activity?

SSA REFERS TO THE PERSON applying for disability as the *claimant*. A claimant is not automatically disqualified from receiving disability benefits just because they are working.

However, the claimant's pre-tax earnings must fall below SSA's monthly Substantial Gainful Activity (SGA) limit to be eligible to receive disability.

In 2023, SGA was raised from the 2022 limit of $1,350 to $1,470. SSA specifies a higher SGA amount for statutorily blind individuals and a lower SGA amount for non-blind individuals.

Step 2: Are your impairments severe?

AN IMPAIRMENT IS *severe* when it

1. significantly interferes with the Claimant's ability to perform either physical (E.g., walking) or mental (E.g., multitasking) work activities; ***and***

2. is expected to last at least 12 consecutive months or result in death.

If the Claimant's impairment or combination of impairments is found to be severe, then SSA proceed to Step 3.

Step 3: Do Your Impairments Meet or Equal a Listing?

SSA NEXT DETERMINES whether the Claimant has an impairment, or combination of impairments, that meets or medically equals one of SSA's listed impairments.

If the Claimant meets or medically equals a Listing, then SSA will find them to be "disabled" at Step 3.

If the Claimant does not meet or medically equal a Listing, then SSA proceeds to Step 4.

Step 4: Are you able to return to your Past Relevant Work?

SSA DETERMINES WHETHER the Claimant is able to perform his or her Past Relevant Work (PRW). PRW is work that was:

1. performed at SGA levels;

2. performed long enough for the claimant to learn how to do all the duties of the job; *and*

3. performed within the last 15 years.

If SSA determines that the Claimant *can* perform any of their PRW despite the limiting effects of their impairments, then the claimant is found to be "not disabled," and the Step 4 analysis ends. If SSA determines that the Claimant *cannot* perform any of their PRW due to their impairments, they proceed to Step 5.

Step 5: Can you adjust to other work?

IN STEP 5, SSA DETERMINES whether the Claimant is capable of performing other work that exists in significant numbers in the national economy on a regular, consistent basis (8 hours per day, 5 days per week). This finding is based on the Claimant's age and educational background, in addition to the physical and mental limitations caused by their impairments.

If SSA determines that the Claimant can adjust to other work, the Claimant is found to be "not disabled" at the fifth and final step of the Five-Step Sequential Evaluation. If SSA determines that the claimant cannot adjust to other work, then the claimant is found to be "disabled."

There you have it.

That is the roadmap which SSA uses to determine whether or not you will be medically approved for disability benefits.

SSA is always required to go through this Five-Step Sequential Evaluation.

This is the analysis that SSA will use at the Application, during the Reconsideration appeal and at Hearing before the Administrative Law Judge.

All disability decisions are based on this evaluation.

It is as simple as that.

Tip #32: Attorney of Record

YOUR CONFIDENTIALITY and privacy are of the utmost concern.

In order for an attorney or Authorized Representative to have access to your claim or to get any information from SSA on your case, you must complete the SSA-1696, Claimant's Appointment of a Representative form.

Once the SSA-1696 form is completed, dated, and signed by you, your attorney will fax it to the District Office, and will be added to the claims record.

Only once the attorney is added to the record with an SSA-1696 form will SSA be able to release critical case information to your designated attorney. This means that your attorney is now the "Attorney of Record."

It is important to note that your attorney will also need to provide your mother's maiden name, as well as your place of birth and city of birth, before they can be verified as your attorney and have information released to them.

In most cases, not only will the SSA-1696 form be submitted to the District Office, but it will also be submitted with the Fee Agreement that you signed outlining the fees that the attorney will accept if you win your case.

The SSA-827 form, Authorization to Disclose Information to the Social Security Administration, is another critical form that is always submitted to SSA and which is an authorization by you to have your medical providers disclose medical records to the Social Security Administration.

These are the standard forms that Social Security will look for in order to add your attorney to the record. Once again, it is essential that your attorney be added to the record for information to be released to him or her.

Additionally, once your attorney has been added to the record, the Social Security Administration will copy them on all the forms that they send to your home.

This is very important since you want your attorney to get a copy of all the forms that are sent to your home. If the attorney gets a copy of the forms that you receive, he or she will make sure that you complete the forms, attend your Consultative Examinations and even assist you in completing the forms for the Social Security Administration.

Remember, they will only receive the forms if they are the attorney listed on the record.

Once you fax in the attorney of record forms to your SSA District Office, always go ahead and call the District Office to make sure that they have received the forms and that they are processing the forms so that your selected attorney can be added to the record.

Tip #33: Submit the SSA-827 Forms

AS PART OF YOUR APPLICATION process, the Social Security District Office will need to request all of your medical records from your medical providers. Because of HIPAA rules and confidentiality rules which were designed to protect you, your medical providers will not release the information to SSA without a signed authorization form.

The SSA-827, Authorization to Disclose Information to the Social Security Administration, is a form that is specifically designed to allow you to sign in the date and allow the Social Security Administration to request your medical records. You must sign and submit this form as part of your application process so that the Social Security Administration can request the necessary medical records.

SSA will use the SSA-827 form multiple times and request medical records from all hospitals, primary care physicians, clinics, and any other medical provider that you have seen in the last three years.

Usually, medical records that are five years or older are archived in the medical record systems and are unavailable. But keep in mind that medical records older than three years have very little value, unless you're claiming that your onset date was at least 5 years ago.

The Social Security Administration really wants to see updated medical records. Generally, anything over 5 years is considered stale and has very little persuasive value when it comes to helping you get approved for your disability benefits.

It should also be noted that there is a "witness" signature line on the SSA-827 Form. If possible, you should have a "witness" be present when you sign the form, and then have the witness sign it and return it.

Make sure that you submit the SSA-827 form to the SSA District Office and the Disability Determination Services so that SSA can request your medical records in a timely fashion.

Of course, you naturally want to make sure that your DDS worker also has a list of your recent medical providers, so that he/she can request the records.

This is a very important component that should not be overlooked.

Remember: DDS can't request your medical records with the SSA 827-Form, unless they know specifically who has been treating you and providing you with medical care.

Tip #34: Comprehensive List of Doctors

AT THE APPLICATION and Reconsideration level, Disability Determination Services, DDS, will request all your medical records so that they can be considered when reviewing your claim for benefits.

As part of your Application process, it is essential that you provide SSA with the name of the facility, the name of the doctor, the address, the telephone number, as well as the dates of service so that all the medical records can be requested.

Suppose you have new doctors that you've gone to and visited or who have treated you for your medical condition. In that case, you want to provide that new information to SSA and/or DDS. The best way to do that is to write them on a piece of paper listing the name of the facility, the name of the doctor, the address, and the telephone number and fax number.

Now, let's be clear.

SSA does not need to have the name of your dentist, for example, unless you are alleging that you have some disability related to your teeth. SSA only needs the information from your doctors that are rendering services to you for your disabling condition. That can include hospitals, doctors, physical therapists, mental health professionals, and even chiropractors or acupuncturists. SSA needs that information.

If they don't have the necessary contact information, then they can't request the medical records. If they don't have the medical records, they can't approve your case. So, as you can now see, we must keep SSA updated with all of the pertinent information relating to your medical providers.

Once this information is submitted, you then want to call the Disability Determination Services case analyst who is working on your case and confirm that they have received your updated list of doctors and medical providers. Don't come crying after the fact that they didn't collect all the medical records. You should have plenty of time to sit down and draft a list of all your doctors so that all the medical records can be timely and easily requested and reviewed.

I have mentioned before that you need to also be an advocate for yourself. Meaning, that sometimes, DDS WILL request the records, but your doctor fails to respond to the medical records request. You have 2 options:

1. Contact your medical provider and make sure they timely respond to the medical records request, or
2. Go to your patient portal and download the documents and send them yourself directly to the DDS worker by fax.

Always make sure you provide SSA with a comprehensive list of doctors, and their contact information. And, regularly update it, as needed.

Tip #35: Updated Medications

AS MENTIONED IN AN earlier chapter, Social Security wants to see that you are a partner in your own health.

Having said that, it is essential that you follow the medication regimen that was prescribed to you by your medical provider. Sometimes, since the application process or the Reconsideration process is so long, it could happen that the medications you were prescribed many months ago might have changed, or the dosage might have increased since you started the application process.

The best thing to do is to write down the updated names of the medication(s) and the prescribing doctor, and the dosage amounts on a piece of paper and fax it to the Disability Determination Services analyst who is working on your case.

You should then call your DDS analyst to confirm that they received the updated medications. Remember, listing down what medications you are taking, as well as the dosage amounts, is an important part of the medical record and should not be overlooked.

You should also bring the list of medications to your SSA Consultative Examination, which may be scheduled for you with an SSA doctor.

The SSA doctor WILL ask for your medication list, and it is good to have it prepared and ready to go. It should be noted that not only will SSA look at the medications which were prescribed to you by your treating physician, but there are also many side effects of certain medications, which need to be considered by Social Security in order to determine if, in fact, you are disabled and eligible for benefits.

Only by updating Disability Determination Services (or the SSA Judge) with your new medications can you be certain that your case has been properly reviewed in order for them to decide your claim for benefits.

It is also important to note, that I would list out any medication side effects that you may be experiencing. It isn't just about the names and dosage amounts of your medication, but it is also about the side effects that are caused from the medications.

So, always make sure that you provide Social Security with your updated medication lists.

If you suffer from headaches, it is helpful to provide DDS with a headaches log.

If you suffer from seizures or asthma attacks, it is also helpful to provide DDS with these home-made logs.

If you don't have a home log available, you can easily download a sample off of the internet.

Tip #36: Updating DDS

AT THE BEGINNING OF your application process, you provided the Social Security Administration with all your medical provider names, including any hospitals, therapists, or other treating sources.

As you know, since the disability eligibility or appeals process can take many months, it is good to keep track of the different medical providers you see during this time. During those months, you will surely be continuously visiting the doctor.

At each of those visits, you may be taking new tests, new laboratory blood samples, new X-rays, new MRIs, or any other type of specialty test which is needed for your body. It is essential that you provide updated test results to the Disability Determination Services. Why? So, SSA can make sure that they are reviewing the most updated results and medical records.

I cannot tell you how many times clients come to me who were not represented at the application level by an attorney and complained that DDS did not review their complete medical records. I asked them if they provided Social Security with updated medical records, and they said "no." Remember that it is your job to inform your attorney and to inform the Social Security Disability Determination Services if new tests have been performed. Social Security will request those test results and will add them to the medical record exhibit file that they can review to determine if you are disabled or not.

So, make sure that you always update Social Security with recent test results.

Tip #37: Clear Out Your Voicemail

KEEP IN MIND THAT YOUR disability attorney is your partner in helping you win your disability case.

It is essential that your attorney (or SSA or DDS!) is able to contact you and communicate with you regarding updates on your case and/or any necessary actions that you need to take. This is how your case will move to the next stage in the eligibility or appeals process.

One of the most frustrating things for an attorney is not being able to get in touch with you, the client.

Often, I have to call a client with the need to get essential information only to find out that the voicemailbox is full or not set up and unable to accept any new calls.

This is a very simple tip.

Just make sure you set up your voicemail, and clear out your voice mailbox regularly so that your doctors, your attorneys, and Social Security can reach you - at any time.

You cannot expect to win your case, if we cannot get you on the telephone.

Tip #38: You Can Work Part-Time

MANY PEOPLE COME TO me and ask me how they will be able to live and support themselves while they're <u>waiting</u> for their application to get approved. Additionally, people come to me <u>after</u> being approved for disability benefits and tell me that the disability benefit check is not enough. They want to work part-time.

So, the question then becomes, "Are *you able to work part-time and still collect disability benefits?*" And the answer to that question is yes, sort of. What do I mean by that? I mean that you must understand how Social Security calculates "income" and "Substantial Gainful Activity."

There are two kinds of income: "earned income" and "unearned income." Earned income is when you roll your sleeves up and go to work every day to earn your paycheck. Unearned income is when you sit at home and receive money in the form of alimony, child support, workers' compensation payments, etc. This means that you are receiving income for unearned work.

Social Security labels income from "working" as Substantial Gainful Activity, which is calculated at $1,470/month in 2023. That means that, under a strict reading of the law, you can work part-time while you are <u>waiting</u> for SSA to make a decision on your application, as long as you "earn" less than $1,470/ month (in 2023) and still be approved.

It is important to always consult with an attorney to make sure that you are not earning more income than allowed when you are working part-time. But, the bottom line is that as long as you are earning less than SGA (under $1,470 a month in 2023), you can work part-time while waiting for a determination to be made on your application.

Once you get approved for benefits, however, there is a different analysis.

It should be noted that there is a concept called "Trial Work Period," where a beneficiary can receive Social Security disability benefits on the basis of his or her own earnings history and may test his or her ability to work and still be considered disabled. SSA does not consider services performed during the trial work period as showing that the disability has ended until services have been performed in at least 9 months (not necessarily consecutive) in a rolling 60-month period. In 2023, this monthly amount will increase to $1,050. The trial work period does not apply to SSI benefits.

You must consult your local SSA District Office about "trial work" so that you are sure that you don't go over the income limits.

SSA also offers a "Ticket to Work" program for those individuals who have already been approved, but still want to work part-time.

Always consult your local SSA District Office before engaging in any type of work (part-time or full-time), so that you are clear on the rules.

Tip #39: Terminal Illnesses

WE HAVE PREVIOUSLY discussed the 5-Step Sequential Evaluation for Determining Disability.

You may recall that Step 2 of the 5-Step analysis is:

"Do you have a severe impairment that *is expected to last 12 or more months and/or result in death*?"

This doesn't necessarily mean that your medical condition has already lasted for 12 months. It means that the medical condition *is expected* to last for a continuous period of not less than 12 or more months, at the very least. Let's give some examples.

In the opening chapters, we gave an example of someone injured while skiing and breaking their leg is most probably not going to be out of work for 12 or more months. Someone who was in a motor vehicle accident and only sustained minor injuries will probably not be out of work for 12 or more months. Both of these examples are cases that would not be eligible for disability benefits.

Remember, you must have a medical condition that has lasted 12 months and/or is expected to last 12 or more months and/or may result in death. Having said that, let's assume someone has terrible pains in their body, and they go to their medical provider. The doctor gives them terrible news that they have cancer or another terminal illness. More concerning is that they are told that they will have to have chemotherapy and radiation treatments that will last several months, even up to a year.

This is a perfect example of a medical condition that is expected to last 12 or more months, even though they were just diagnosed yesterday. They can still apply for disability benefits with cancer since their medical condition is expected to last 12 or more months.

Similarly, there is a whole list of medical conditions that are expected to last 12 or more months, which will allow you to get approved prior to waiting the actual 12 months. These are called "TERI" cases.

TERI (Terminal Illness) or Compassionate Allowance Cases are automatically approved without having to wait 12 or more months. The current list of carrying cases includes the following:

A

- Acute Leukaemia

- Adrenal Cancer — With Distant Metastases or Inoperable, Unresectable, or Recurrent

- Adult Non-Hodgkin Lymphoma

- Adult-Onset Huntington Disease

- Aicardi-Goutieres Syndrome

- Alexander Disease (Alx) — Neonatal And Infantile

- Allan-Herndon-Dudley Syndrome

- Alobar Holoprosencephaly

- Alpers Disease

- Alpha Mannosidosis — Type Ii And Iii

- Als/Parkinsonism Dementia Complex

- Alstrom Syndrome

- Alveolar Soft Part Sarcoma

- Amegakaryocytic Thrombocytopenia

- Amyotrophic Lateral Sclerosis (Als)

- Anaplastic Adrenal Cancer — Adult With Distant Metastases Or Inoperable, Unresectable, or Recurrent

- Angelman Syndrome

- Angiosarcoma

- Aortic Atresia

- Aplastic Anemia

- Astrocytoma — Grade Iii And Iv

- Ataxia Telangiectasia

- Atypical Teratoid/Rhabdoid Tumor

B

- Batten Disease

- Beta Thalassemia Major

- Bilateral Optic Atrophy — Infantile

- Bilateral Retinoblastoma

- Bladder Cancer — With Distant Metastases Or Inoperable Or Unresectable

C

- Canavan Disease (Cd)

- Cach — Vanishing White Matter Disease-Infantile And Childhood Onset Forms

- Carcinoma Of Unknown Primary Site

- Cardiac Amyloidosis — Al Type

- Caudal Regression Syndrome — Types Iii And Iv

- Cdkl5 Deficiency Disorder (Effective 08/19/2019)

- Cerebro Oculo Facio Skeletal (Cofs) Syndrome

- Cerebrotendinous Xanthomatosis

- Child Lymphoblastic Lymphoma

- Child Lymphoma

- Child Neuroblastoma — with Distant Metastases or Recurrent

- Chondrosarcoma — With Multimodal Therapy

- Chronic Idiopathic Intestinal Pseudo Obstruction

- Chronic Myelogenous Leukemia (CML) — Blast Phase

- Coffin-Lowry Syndrome

- Congenital Lymphedema

- Congenital Myotonic Dystrophy

- Cornelia De Lange Syndrome — Classic Form

- Corticobasal Degeneration

- Creutzfeldt-Jakob Disease (CJD) — Adult

- Cri Du Chat Syndrome

D

- Degos Disease — Systemic

- Desanctis Cacchione Syndrome

- Dravet Syndrome

E

- Early-Onset Alzheimer's Disease

- Edwards Syndrome (Trisomy 18)

- Feisenmenger Syndrome

- Endometrial Stromal Sarcoma

- Endomyocardial Fibrosis

- Ependymoblastoma (Child Brain Cancer)

- Erdheim Chester Disease

- Esophageal Cancer

- Esthesioneuroblastoma

- Ewing Sarcoma

F

- Farber Disease (Fd) — Infantile

- Fatal Familial Insomnia

- Fibrodysplasia Ossificans Progressiva

- Fibrolamellar Cancer

- Follicular Dendritic Cell Sarcoma — Metastatic Or Recurrent

- Friedreichs Ataxia (Frda)

- Frontotemporal Dementia (FTD), Picks Disease-Type A — Adult

- Fryns Syndrome

- Fucosidosis — Type 1

- Fukuyama Congenital Muscular Dystrophy

- Fulminant Giant Cell Myocarditis

G

- Galactosialidosis — Early And Late Infantile Types

- Gallbladder Cancer

- Gaucher Disease (Gd) — Type 2

- Giant Axonal Neuropathy

- Glioblastoma Multiforme (Brain Cancer)

- Glioma Grade Iii And Iv

- Glutaric Acidemia — Type II

H

- Head And Neck Cancers — With Distant Metastasis Or Inoperable Or Unresectable

- Heart Transplant Graft Failure

- Heart Transplant Wait List — 1a/1b

- Hemophagocytic Lymphohistiocytosis (Hlh) — Familial Type

- Hepatoblastoma

- Hepatopulmonary Syndrome

- Hepatorenal Syndrome

- Histiocytosis Syndromes

- Hoyeaal-Hreidarsson Syndrome

- Hutchinson-Gilford Progeria Syndrome

- Hydranencephaly

- Hypocomplementemia Urticarial Vasculitis Syndrome

- Hypophosphatasia Perinatal (Lethal) And Infantile Onset Types

- Hypoplastic Left Heart Syndrome

I

- I Cell Disease

- Idiopathic Pulmonary Fibrosis

- Infantile Free Sialic Acid Storage Disease

- Infantile Neuroaxonal Dystrophy (INAD)

- Infantile Neuronal Ceroid Lipofuscinoses

- Inflammatory Breast Cancer (IBC)

- Intracranial Hemangiopericytoma

J

- Jervell And Lange-Nielsen Syndrome

- Joubert Syndrome

- Junctional Epidermolysis Bullosa — Lethal Type

- Juvenile Onset Huntington's Disease

K

- Kidney Cancer — Inoperable Or Unresectable

- Kleefstra Syndrome

- Krabbe Disease (Kd) — Infantile

- Kufs Disease — Type A And B

L

- Large Intestine Cancer — With Distant Metastasis Or Inoperable, Unresectable, or Recurrent

- Late Infantile Neuronal Ceroid Lipofuscinoses

- Leigh's Disease

- Leiomyosarcoma

- Leptomeningeal Carcinomatosis

- Lesch-Nyhan Syndrome (LNS)

- Lewy Body Dementia

- Liposarcoma — Metastatic or Recurrent

- Lissencephaly

- Liver Cancer

- Lowe Syndrome

- Lymphomatoid Granulomatosis — Grade III

M

- Malignant Brain Stem Gliomas — Childhood

- Malignant Ectomesenchymoma

- Malignant Gastrointestinal Stromal Tumor

- Malignant Germ Cell Tumor

- Malignant Multiple Sclerosis

- Malignant Renal Rhabdoid Tumor

- Mantle Cell Lymphoma (MCL)

- Maple Syrup Urine Disease

- Marshall-Smith Syndrome

- Mastocytosis — Type IV

- Mecp2 Duplication Syndrome

- Medulloblastoma — With Metastases

- Megacystis Microcolon Intestinal Hypoperistalsis Syndrome

- Megalencephaly Capillary Malformation Syndrome

- Menkes Disease — Classic Or Infantile Onset Form

- Merkel Cell Carcinoma — With Metastases

- Merosin Deficient Congenital Muscular Dystrophy

- Metachromatic Leukodystrophy (MLD) — Late Infantile

- Mitral Valve Atresia

- Mixed Dementias

- MPS I, Formerly Known As Hurler Syndrome

- Mps Ii, Formerly Known As Hunter Syndrome

- Mps Iii, Formerly Known As Sanfilippo Syndrome

- Mucosal Malignant Melanoma

- Multicentric Castleman Disease

- Multiple System Atrophy

- Myoclonic Epilepsy With Ragged Red Fibers Syndrome

N

- Neonatal Adrenoleukodystrophy

- Nephrogenic Systemic Fibrosis

- Neurodegeneration With Brain Iron Accumulation — Types 1 And 2

- Nfu-1 Mitochondrial Disease

- Niemann-Pick Disease (NPD) — Type A

- Niemann-Pick Disease-Type C

- Nonketotic Hyperglycinemia

- Non-Small Cell Lung Cancer

O

- Obliterative Bronchiolitis

- Ohtahara Syndrome

- Oligodendroglioma Brain Cancer — Grade III

- Ornithine Transcarbamylase (Otc) Deficiency

- Orthochromatic Leukodystrophy With Pigmented Glia

- Osteogenesis Imperfecta (Oi) — Type II

- Osteosarcoma, Formerly Known As Bone Cancer — With Distant Metastases Or Inoperable Or Unresectable

- Ovarian Cancer — With Distant Metastases Or Inoperable Or Unresectable

P

- Pallister-Killian Syndrome

- Pancreatic Cancer

- Paraneoplastic Pemphigus

- Patau Syndrome (Trisomy 13)

- Pearson Syndrome

- Pelizaeus-Merzbacher Disease-Classic Form

- Pelizaeus-Merzbacher Disease-Connatal Form

- Peripheral Nerve Cancer — Metastatic Or Recurrent

- Peritoneal Mesothelioma

- Peritoneal Mucinous Carcinomatosis

- Perry Syndrome

- Phelan-Mcdermid Syndrome

- Pitt Hopkins Syndrome (Effective 08/19/2019)

- Pleural Mesothelioma

- Pompe Disease — Infantile

- Primary Central Nervous System Lymphoma

- Primary Effusion Lymphoma

- Primary Peritoneal Cancer (Effective 08/19/2019)

- Primary Progressive Aphasia

- Progressive Bulbar Palsy

- Progressive Multifocal Leukoencephalopathy

  Progressive Supranuclear Palsy

- Prostate Cancer — Hormone Refractory Disease — or with Visceral Metastases

  Pulmonary Atresia

- Pulmonary Kaposi Sarcoma

R

- Retinopathy Of Prematurity — Stage V

- Rett (RTT) Syndrome

- Revesz Syndrome

- Rhabdomyosarcoma

- Rhizomelic Chondrodysplasia Punctata

- Richter Syndrome (Effective 08/19/2019)

- Roberts Syndrome

S

- Salivary Cancers

- Sandhoff Disease

- Schindler Disease — Type 1

- Seckel Syndrome

- Severe Combined Immunodeficiency — Childhood

- Single Ventricle

- Sinonasal Cancer

- Sjogren-Larsson Syndrome

- Skin Malignant Melanoma With Metastases

- Small Cell Cancer (Large Intestine, Prostate, or Thymus)

- Small Cell Cancer Of The Female Genital Tract

- Small Cell Lung Cancer

- Small Intestine Cancer — With Distant Metastases or Inoperable, Unresectable, or Recurrent

- Smith Lemli Opitz Syndrome

- Soft Tissue Sarcoma — With Distant Metastases Or Recurrent

- Spinal Muscular Atrophy (Sma) — Types 0 And 1

- Spinal Nerve Root Cancer-Metastatic Or Recurrent

- Spinocerebellar Ataxia

- Stiff Person Syndrome

- Stomach Cancer — With Distant Metastases Or Inoperable, Unresectable, or Recurrent

- Subacute Sclerosing Panencephalitis

- Superficial Siderosis Of The Central Nervous System

T

- Tabes Dorsalis

- Tay Sachs Disease — Infantile Type

- Tetrasomy 18p

- Thanatophoric Dysplasia — Type 1

- Thyroid Cancer

- Transplant Coronary Artery Vasculopathy

- Tricuspid Atresia

U

- Ullrich Congenital Muscular Dystrophy

- Ureter Cancer — With Distant Metastases Or Inoperable, Unresectable, or Recurrent

- Usher Syndrome — Type I

V

- Ventricular Assist Device Recipient — Left, Right, Or Biventricular

W

- Walker Warburg Syndrome

- Wolf-Hirschhorn Syndrome

- Wolman Disease

X

- X-Linked Lymphoproliferative Disease

- X-Linked Myotubular Myopathy

- Xeroderma Pigmentosum

Z

- Zellweger Syndrome

I send my prayers and blessings to all of you who do not feel well and hope you never have to apply as a TERI application.

Just know that your application can be expedited for quick approval if you are a candidate for a TERI case. Consult your attorney on how to alert SSA if you meet the TERI criteria.

Tip #40: Long-Term Disability Benefits

IT IS IMPORTANT TO note that many of my clients have Long-Term Disability (LTD) policies with private insurance carriers.

Be advised that your Social Security application for disability benefits may impact your long-term disability policies. It may be impacted in two different ways.

The first way is that the payments you receive from the Social Security disability benefits may offset any payments that you're receiving for the long-term disability policy. Meaning if you're receiving $1,000 a month from Social Security, it may result in a reduction of your long-term disability policy payments by $1,000 a month...which is called an offset.

Another important thing to keep in consideration is the impact that your back benefits receive from Social Security and how they may potentially play into your LTD policy.

We already know that with an SSDI case, it is possible to go retroactive 12 months before the application date and claim your disability. As such, by the time you get approved, you may have accumulated 12, 18, 24, or 36 months of benefits, which are due to you. Those are called back benefits. Some long-term disability insurance carriers have written into their policy that you must reimburse the LTD carrier if you receive a back payment from the SSA.

This means that if you receive a big award of $10,000, $20,000, $30,000, or $40,000 because of accumulated back pay, you may have to give the entire lump sum payment to the LTD carrier.

As such, if you have a long-term disability policy with a private insurance carrier, you must read the fine print on your policy to determine if 1) your disability payments from Social Security will result in an offset of your monthly payments and 2) if you will have to repay back the back pay to the private insurance carrier.

Please be aware that long-term disability policies do play a surprising role when mingled together with SSDI payments and back payments.

Tip #41: Jail time

THERE IS A FAMOUS JOKE that goes like this....

The Jail Warden asks the death row inmate what he would like as his last meal.

The inmate replies, *"Strawberries."*

Warden says, *"But strawberries are out of season for 6 months."*

The inmate replies, *"I'll wait!"*

Yes, from time to time, my clients have told me that they've either been incarcerated or spent time in prison. And they want to know if that will affect their benefits.

Let's first take a step back. If you have an open warrant for your arrest, you cannot collect Social Security Disability Insurance. Social Security will consider you a fleeing felon and ineligible for their benefits if you have an outstanding arrest warrant specifically for fleeing prosecution or confinement on a felony charge. Under federal law, you cannot get Social Security benefits if you are fleeing to avoid prosecution for a felony OR violating the terms of probation or parole.

That means that if you have an open warrant for your arrest, you must FIRST resolve that open warrant with the proper authorities before you can collect your disability benefits. Jail time also plays a role in your inability to collect disability benefits for a specific period of time. You cannot obtain disability benefits during the time that you are incarcerated.

However, all hope is not lost because you can request medical records from the prison infirmary or hospital and submit them to Social Security for review to see if you are disabled or not. But during the time you were in jail, you could not receive disability benefits.

Make sure you tell your attorney if you spent any time in jail or prison so that your attorney knows whether he or she needs to collect the medical records during the time that you were imprisoned.

Tip #42: Electronic Fillings

You have the option to either file your SSDI application online at www.ssa.gov or submit the application in paper form by having an appointment with the Social Security Administration. At this time, you can only file a complete application online for Social Security Disability Insurance. All Supplemental Security Income applications, on the other hand, can be initiated online, but the rest of the application must be completed with your local SSA District Office.

The easiest way to complete an SSI application is either to download the application from the internet, complete it, and then return it to the local SSA District Office, or set up an appointment with a local SSA District Office to complete the application during a scheduled phone interview with a Social Security worker.

It is worth noting that if your application is denied, you can request the Reconsideration either online at www.ssa.gov[1] or print it online, complete it, and fax it to your local District Office. If you prefer the latter, make sure that you keep a fax receipt and the certified mail a copy of the request for Reconsideration.

You can request a hearing before an Administrative Law Judge online at www.sss.gov[2] if your Reconsideration is denied. It is a simple process that requires you to log in to ssa.gov, put in your basic information, and request a hearing before a Judge online.

If your hearing decision is not in your favor and you are denied benefits, you can appeal electronically to Social Security Appeals Council at www.ssa.gov[3]. Again, you have the option to submit it physically to the local District Office.

It is important to mention that you only have 60 calendar days to ask for an appeal after you were denied. So, keep an eye on your calendar.

---

1. http://www.ssa.gov

2. http://www.sss.gov

3. http://www.ssa.gov

In conclusion, you have a choice to ask for an appeal or hearing electronically or physically, depending on what is easier for you.

I would suggest you use digital means as you will get results fast, and you will get an online confirmation of the filing. Faxing the appeal might take a week for the Social Security office to catch up on their long list of faxes that still have to be processed.

Always print out the electronic receipt from the computer of your appeal and keep it in your records!

Tip #43: Don't Yell – Ever!

There's a famous joke that's told about a janitor who jumped out of the closet to surprise some of his coworkers. When he jumped out of the closet, he screamed out the words at the top of his voice: "*Supplies*," get it? Not a surprise — but "*supplies*."

I know, it's a corny joke!

We might think sometimes that when we raise our voices, it makes us more powerful or it helps our words to be heard. But in reality, all it does is frustrate and anger the listener.

Throughout this book, we've discussed many times how the Social Security Administration has multiple departments that process your claim.

There's the District Office, which processes claims for SSI and SSDI. The local Social Security District Office will process your name, date of birth, Social Security number, and address, as well as whether or not you have enough credits. They will also perform an income and resource check on you to see if you qualify for the SSI program.

The Social Security office will assign a case manager to your claim. This case manager must be treated with respect. If you want your case to be timely processed. If there is an error in the processing of your case, it's best to let your attorney handle the error and straighten it out with the Social Security office. Yelling should never be an option when dealing with Social Security Administration, as it will just anger and frustrate them. And possibly even cause them to hang up the phone on you.

As we've also discussed, the Social Security office will split your case and will send the medical portion of your file to the local Disability Determination Services office. The disability determination office will also assign a case manager to work on your case. This case manager is responsible for obtaining the names of your medical providers, the addresses of your medical providers, the phone numbers and fax numbers of your medical providers, as well as the dates of service.

The Disability Determination Services worker will also send you forms to complete that you must return in order for your case to be timely processed. The DDS office will also schedule your Consultative Examination to be examined by one of the Social Security doctors. It may be frustrating at times to get a hold of the disability determination service worker who has been assigned your case. But you must remember that when you finally speak to them that you must be professional and courteous.

Once again, yelling will never get the job done. Many people think that by yelling, they become more powerful. But as we have already said, this does not help resolve the situation. And it's best to let your attorney deal with the DDS worker.

In conclusion, and I cannot emphasize enough times, it is important to remember that there are several partnerships going on over here during the process of your case.

There is a partnership between you and the Social Security Administration. There's a partnership between you and Disability Determination Services. Also, there's a partnership between you and your medical provider. There's a partnership between you and your attorney. And, finally, there is a partnership between you and yourself.

As you go along the disability journey, at no point along the way should you ever raise your voice or yell at any of your partners!

It's just not worth it.

It doesn't give you power and will only upset and destroy your relationship with the other party who is on the receiving end of your outburst!

Stay cool and stay professional!

Tip #44: The Award Letter

If you've done everything correctly and your medical records support a favorable decision, your case will be approved in a timely fashion.

You will be notified by receiving an SSA Award Letter from your Social Security District Office. Your Award Letter is the official stamp which means that your case has been approved. It will also contain other important information in your award letter, like back pay information, information relating to Medicare benefits, how much (if anything) is owed to your attorney and other essential information. In addition, the date of when your onset when your disability began, your entitlement date for when your benefits begin, as well as the payment schedule, will be mentioned.

If you disagree with the dates of the award letter, meaning you disagree as to when Social Security determined that your disability began, you have 60 days to appeal this decision. The appeal process, once again, will take several months. So, serious thought has to be put into whether or not you feel you should appeal your onset date or not.

If you disagree with the payment schedule or the payment amount, you can call your local SSA District Office to have them calculate and confirm your benefits amount. Your Primary Insurance Amount (PIA, which we have already spoken about) is the benefit amount you'll receive each and every month based on your averaged earnings paid over the course of your career. In most cases, this number is correct and cannot be adjusted higher. Once again. If you disagree, you can appeal.

Be advised that SSI and SSDI are two different programs. As previously mentioned, the SSI payments will be coming from the local Social Security District Office. Whereas the SSDI payments will be coming from the SSA Payment Center in Baltimore.

If you have difficulty obtaining your payments in a timely fashion, you should work with your attorney to contact the local SSA District Office or the SSA Payment Center in order to follow up on the award letter to make sure that you receive all of your payments.

You may also recall, as part of the application process, the Social Security Administration asked you if you wanted to have a direct deposit of the awards once you were found disabled. If you already provided your banking information, your bank account number, and routing number, then you should receive an auto payment directly into your accounts. Otherwise, you will receive a hard check in the mail. If you wish to receive a direct deposit into your accounts but neglected to provide Social Security with the banking number, the banking information, the bank account, and the routing number. You can still call the Social Security Administration and provide that information to them.

The award letter will also mention if you are awarded Medicaid with your SSI, or Medicare with your SSDI, this is all important information. And the award letters should be held in a safe, secure place in case you need to reference them in the future.

If you received your award letter, it means that you won your case.

In all cases, SSI payments will not be put into pay status until you complete a short interview called the Pre-Effectuation Review Contact, or the PERC, for short. The PERC interview is a simple 15-minute telephone interview with your local SSA District Office so that they can determine if you have had any major changes since you first filed for your application. For instance, did you get married or divorced? Did you have any more children? Have your living conditions changed? The PERC interview must be completed before you get paid. It can take 30 days after you receive your Award Letter to schedule a PERC appointment, so make a note on your calendar to follow up with the District Office.

The SSDI payments are processed in Baltimore, Maryland, and not at your local SSA District Office. Since no PERC is required, it is usually a quicker process to get paid on an SSDI claim.

Tip #45: CLAIMANT, not APPLICANT

As we move through the Social Security process, terms and definitions are important to understand.

It should be noted that people often refer to themselves as the *applicant*, but that is not the proper term that SSA uses.

Social Security describes the person listed on the application as a *Claimant*, not an "*applicant*." The reason for that is that you are filing a "*claim*" for benefits.

You remain the Claimant from the beginning of the process to the end of the process.

When calling the Social Security Administration, they will ask you the name of the Claimant, not the applicant. When you go before the Judge, the Judge will refer to you as the Claimant and not the applicant. Each person is entitled to due process of law, which requires notice before any action is taken.

Understanding the definitions and terms used by the Social Security Administration is essential for effective communication.

Only once you are approved are you now referred to as a *beneficiary* and not the *Claimant*.

Tip # 46: District Offices Versus Hearing Offices

It is important to note that there's a distinction between the local Social Security District Office and the Office of Hearings and Operations (OHO).

The local SSA District Offices are responsible, as we've said before, for processing your application, your Reconsideration, and your Request for a Hearing before an Administrative Law Judge. But they do not hold the actual hearings in the local District Office. The hearings are held at the Office of Hearings and Operations. The Judges, as well as their clerks and their assistants, are in a completely separate physical location which is called the OHO.

Once the Judge receives the complete file from the local District Office, the ball is in his or her court. The Judge will conduct a hearing and continue to build the file. The Judge will also issue a decision as to whether the case is approved or denied. Once a decision is made by the Judge, the Judge will then send a medical decision to you. The District Office, on the other hand, will mail you an SSA Award letter or letter stating that the benefits have been denied.

Local District Offices generally closed at 4:00 PM every day, whereas Offices of Hearing and Operations generally close at 5:00 PM every day. They also have different phone numbers, as they are in different locations. It's always best to work with your attorney, but it's important for you to know the difference between the local District Office and the Office of Hearings and Operations.

Tip #47: No Attorney Fee, Unless You Win

One of the greatest things about hiring a Social Security disability attorney is that you don't have to pay any fee, unless you win your Social Security disability case.

In what other industry is this type of fee arrangement prevalent?

Anytime you call a plumber, electrician, or dentist, they will ask you for a fee. Only in the case of disability attorneys there is no fee unless the case is approved and you are awarded benefits.

In almost all cases, the fee will be 25% of your back benefits from your first check, but it won't be more than $7,200. All of the awards are approved by the Social Security Administration Commissioner prior to disbursement.

You don't have to pay the fee once you receive your back-pay award, as the Social Security Administration, in almost all cases, will forward the attorney fees directly from the award to the attorney prior to releasing the money to you. Mostly, it will be directly deposited to the attorney, once the case is processed by the US Treasury or the local District Office.

In some cases, when multiple attorneys represent the client, there may be a dispute about who gets more than the other. In such cases, a Fee Petition is required and must be approved by the District Office and/or the Administrative Law Judge. Part of the Fee Petition process requires that each attorney list the services they provided, the dates they were provided, and the time spent on the service. So, the Judge will split the award fairly according to their effort.

For instance, you may have one attorney who only put in two hours, but the other attorney put in 10 hours. The fee petition will break down those hours of service performed by each attorney, and divide the legal fees accordingly.

Remember, you won't lose anything by hiring a Social Security disability attorney to assist you with your claim or appeal for benefits.

There is should never be any upfront costs or payments to any disability attorney. Only if the case is approved.

So, if you win your case, that would be the only time you have to pay the attorney. While this may not seem like a "tip" about how to get approved, it really is...

What is that tip or word of advice?

HIRE AN ATTORNEY IF YOU WANT TO INCREASE YOUR CHANCES OF GETTING YOUR CLAIM FOR BENEFITS APPROVED.

Tip #48: Four Places

The Social Security disability process is a lengthy process. And, to many of you, it is also a confusing process where many of you get lost along the way.

In general, your application is always in one of four different locations.

The first place your application can be is at your local SSA District Office. When you apply for benefits, the local District Office is responsible for confirming your name, address, birth date, Social Security number, citizenship status, and work credits, if any. There are many Social Security case managers, and your case has to be assigned to a case manager before it will be worked on.

Secondly, your case may be at the Disability Determination Services or DDS. The role of DDS is to process the medical portion of your case. DDS is responsible for requesting all medical records from your treating providers for scheduling consultative examinations with the Social Security doctors, sending out function and work history reports, and determining if they feel you are medically disabled.

The eligibility process can take anywhere from four to eight months, depending on your number of medical providers. Remember, if you have four doctors and three hospitals, you would have seven medical providers altogether. DDS will not decide on your application until they receive the medical records from all seven providers. They will also not decide on your application if they've ordered a Consultative Examination or if you haven't returned the forms they sent you.

Once DDS makes a medical determination, they will send it back to the District Office to mail out to you either a denial letter or an award letter.

If you case is denied, you will need to Request a Reconsideration appeal. If the Reconsideration is denied, then the case will end up before the Judge.

The Office of Hearing and Operations (OHO) is the office where the hearings are held with the Administrative Law Judge. If your Application and Reconsideration is denied, you will have to Request a Hearing Before an Administrative Law Judge, which is processed at the District Office. Once it is processed, it will move to OHO for processing.

The OHO will convert your paper file into an electronic file and upload all of your records into the Electronic Records Express (ERE) so that the Judge and the attorney can review the records. It generally takes anywhere from six to 12 months to receive a hearing date with a Judge. This is the third location where your case may be suspended or held in limbo until a hearing date is set.

The final location where your claim may be is at the Social Security Administration Payment Center in Baltimore, Maryland. The SSA Payment Center is responsible for reviewing the determination that was made on your claim and issuing SSDI payments.

They will calculate the months that you were approved for benefits and issue payment to you.

The SSI award is generally a standard set amount by the state. The payment center processes SSDI awards, and your local SSA District Office processes SSI awards. The payment center is the final stop for your claim, which was approved for benefits and will always result in a payment to you as soon as it is processed.

In most cases, if you provide the SSA District Office with your routing number and bank account number, they will deposit the money straight into your bank account. They would mail you a hard check if you did not provide this information.

In conclusion, there are generally four places where your application may be held in limbo:

1. the local District Office;
2. DDS;
3. OHO, or
4. the SSA Payment Center.

In some cases, there could be a fifth or sixth place where your claim is pending.

The fifth location would be the SSA Appeals Council, which reviews any decision by a Judge which you disagree with. Or, the final and sixth location, Federal District Court, when you appeal the decision made by the SSA Appeals Council, if you still disagree.

Most people get lost in the maze of the process. Knowing the potential locations of your claim for benefits, will assist you in understanding how to locate and resolve any delays you may be having.

Tip #49: Be Respectful to the Judge

The Judge plays a very important role in the outcome of your case. Remember, when you are in court, you are in the Judges kingdom. Therefore, it is important that we pay respect to the Judge throughout the hearing.

The regular face-to-face hearings are held in a courtroom, with the Judge wearing a robe just like you see on television. Yes, they also have a gavel (if they need it). And there is a bailiff who is on-call and ready to jump into action, if necessary. For in-person hearings, it is advised to dress respectfully and not appear in front of the Judge in casual clothing unless you have a medical reason. You want to leave a good impression on the Judge.

Being respectful to the Judge also means that you have to be truthful to the Judge. Therefore, it is recommended never to lie not only because you took an oath or affirmation to tell the truth, because it generally won't help.

I recently had a Claimant who was before the Judge and who was caught in a lie after she took the oath to tell only the truth and nothing but the truth. She said that she didn't work since 2018, when in fact, she worked 2019, 2020, and 2021.

How did the Judge know that she worked? Because the Judge pulled the Earnings Record of the Claimant, which clearly showed earnings. This lie destroyed all credibility with the Judge. You can never ever lie to the Judge. Being respectful to the Judge doesn't only mean to show manners, but it also means that you have to tell the truth.

Moreover, never exaggerate your medical condition because the Judge has already reviewed your medical records. Therefore, embellishing the condition diminishes your credibility, and ultimately, you will be questioned and doubted. There would be chances that your testimonies would be declared fraudulent. Don't forget, your testimony has to match up with the medical records.

I know it seems silly to even say this, but the ONLY way you should ever refer to the Judge is either "Yes, Your Honor," Yes, Sir," or "Yes, Ma'am." Remember, the Judge is not your friend from high school and you can never call the Judge by his/her first name.

It also goes without saying that you should never interrupt the Judge or try to speak over the Judge. That's a no-no!

In conclusion, be respectful to the Judge and always be truthful.

Tip #50: Review Time

Just like in class, it's time for a review.

As previously discussed, there are two primary types of programs which are available for disabled individuals through the Social Security Administration. The first program is Supplemental Security Income (SSI), and the other is Social Security Disability Insurance (SSDI).

The programs mentioned above seem the same, but there are some differences between them, and a person must understand those differences before applying for benefits. Therefore, understanding the basics of the programs is a must.

SSI is a needs-based program only eligible for people who have not worked or accumulated enough work credits.

SSDI, on the other hand, is a program based on work credits earned throughout your career.

In most cases, you need 40 active credits to be eligible for SSDI. The best way to check if you have credits is either to call your local Social Security District Office and ask the representative to tell you if you have enough work credits to apply for Social Security Disability Insurance. At the same time, you can also go to www.ssa.gov[4] and login to determine if you have enough credits to apply for benefits. What other major differences are there between SSI and SSDI?

Benefit Amount:

BENEFIT AMOUNT IS ONE of the main differences between SSI and SSDI. For SSI, the benefit amount is usually based on a predetermined Federal Benefit Amount, and everyone gets the same amount. In 2023, the Federal Benefit Amount is $914 for an individual (and $1,371 for a couple) a month, with little differences in the amount from state to state.

---

4. http://www.ssa.gov

Meanwhile, SSDI is based on an average of how much money you paid to the system. Some of you may have earned minimum wage and paid very little into the program, so your benefit amount would be very low each month if you're awarded benefits. Similarly, suppose some of you have been successful throughout your career. In that case, your benefit amount can be in the thousands every month — so one of the main differences between SSI and SSDI is the benefit amounts.

Benefit and Application Date:

ANOTHER MAJOR DIFFERENCE between SSI and SSDI is in relation to the application date. In the case of SSI, benefits are only paid from the application date forward; no retroactive benefits exist. At the same time, SSDI will allow you to go retroactive one year from the date of application. That means that if you're just discovering the SSDI program now, you can still go retroactive 12 months from the application date and get paid for those months one year before your application date.

Medicaid vs. Medicare:

IF AWARDED SSI, YOU are automatically entitled to Medicaid in most states.

In contrast, SSDI awards all beneficiaries with Medicare after being on the program for 29 months. In this program, a person must wait five months to be eligible for these benefits. Therefore, they must wait 29 months from the onset date of disability, or 24 months from their entitlement date, including the five-month waiting.

In most cases, most people would prefer to receive Medicare; it is one of the advantages of being eligible for the SSDI program.

Auxiliary Benefits

ANOTHER BENEFIT OF SSDI is that all of your children under 18 years old or in school are entitled to children's Auxiliary Benefits. It means that a percentage of your monthly benefit amount is also allocated to your children, and there is no limit on the number of children you have as long as they are under 18. In comparison, SSI does not allow for auxiliary benefits.

Resources

THERE ARE GOING TO be some people who are eligible for both SSI and SSDI. But it will depend on some of the SSI requirements for the program because SSI is a needs-based program. There are resource restrictions. A single person cannot have more than $2,000 in the bank, and a married person cannot have more than $3,000 in the bank as of 2023. It is important to note that your first house, as is your first automobile, is exempt if you live in it.

In contrast, SSDI has no income and resource restrictions. You can have a million dollars in the bank if that's what you have, and it will not impact your SSDI eligibility.

Eligibility and Marriage

KEEPING IN MIND THE income restrictions for SSI, many people ask if they could get married while they're applying for SSI or SSDI. Its answer is not so simple because it depends on your income/resources and your partner's income/resources.

For SSDI, there are no income or resource restrictions. There is no restriction; you can fall in love and marry. Meanwhile, SSI has some restrictions on income and resources. It's important to bear in mind that if you marry someone with a high income or a substantial number of resources, it may affect your eligibility for the SSI program.

In conclusion, before you begin the journey of applying for Social Security Disability benefits, it is important to know the differences between SSI and SSDI. If you're not sure about your eligibility for SSI or SSDI, the best thing to do is either consult with a local District Office or consult with an attorney to help you navigate through the administrative maze.

Payments

HOPEFULLY, YOU WILL be approved for Social Security disability benefits. My goal as an attorney has always been to ensure you get paid. Often, many of you will encounter a delay in receiving your payments. And you need to understand how the payments centers work so that you can expeditiously receive your Social Security Disability benefits.

Because SSI is a needs-based program, the local District Office is responsible for issuing payments for all SSI approval. Therefore, if you're delayed in receiving an SSI payment, you should contact your local District Office and confirm with them if there's anything else you need to do to put your case in the payment mode.

For SSI approval, SSA will require you to perform **PERC** appointments. PERC stands for **Pre-Effectuation Review Contact**. The appointment is required before SSI benefits can be paid. The PERC appointment is an opportunity for the local District Office to check with you to see if there have been any major changes since you first applied for SSI.

They will ask questions like have you gotten married since filing your application? Have you gotten divorced? Have any of your children moved out of the house? Have you had any new children? Did you win the lottery? What changes have happened since you applied it a year and a half ago? Have you worked at all since filing your application? And many others.

As such, you will need to have a PERC telephone call with SSA that will not last longer than 15 minutes, but is necessary as a part of the Social Security payment process for SSI.

In comparison, SSDI payments are processed at the SSA Payments Center in Baltimore, Maryland. If you have not received your money or your approved benefits for SSDI, the local District Office will not be able to help you if the delay is coming from the central payment Centre in Baltimore, Maryland. Unfortunately, the Payment Center will not speak to Claimants unless an attorney represents them. Thus, you will need your attorney to go ahead and call the payment center to help you get paid. If you choose to call the District Office, they will forward the inquiry to the payment Center for processing. Unfortunately, the District Office will play a very small role (if any) in getting the case paid if the case is at the Payment Center.

In conclusion, after applying for benefits and possibly even going through a hearing with a Judge, you want to make sure you get paid after you've been approved. Understanding the payment process and the differences between SSI and SSDI will help you move forward.

Tip #51: Retroactive Benefits

Many people don't realize that it is possible to go retroactive and get paid up to one year from your SSDI application date and capture all of the lost months during that one-year waiting period. Let me explain.

As discussed, two different programs have been set up for disability benefits. The first program is called Supplemental Security Income (SSI), and the second program is called Social Security Disability Insurance (SSDI).

Unfortunately, because the Supplemental Security Income program is a needs-based program, it is impossible to go retroactive before the application date. You can only obtain benefits from the application date moving forward. However, because the Social Security Disability Insurance program is based on work credits, it is possible to go retroactive and get paid for the 12 months prior to the application date.

People don't realize how beneficial this is to them and their wallets.

Since each month has a certain benefit amount value, the more approved months you can collect and get approved for disability benefits, the better it is for you as it will result in a larger benefit amount awarded to you once you're approved for benefits.

You want to try to capture the maximum number of months as part of your application process. Therefore, on all Social Security Disability Insurance applications, I always recommend that my clients go retroactive as far back as possible. Usually, it means that they will go retroactively back to the last date worked when they were earning over Substantial Gainful Activity (SAG), which in 2023 is $1,470.

If, for some reason, you are working and earning over SGA during those 12 retroactive months from the application date, we would only go back as far as when you stopped working or earning above SGA. However, if you haven't worked for the last 12 months before the application date, we can go backward 12 or more months on the Social Security Disability Insurance program.

It is worth noting that there is a five-month eligibility period rule for the Social Security Disability Insurance program before you can collect benefits. that means you do not get paid for the program's first five months.

Having said that, if you only go retroactive for 12 months, and then you need five months of an eligibility period, the award will only be for seven of those retroactive months, not 12.

Therefore, using an alleged onset date of 17 months prior to the application date is ideal since Social Security will only pay 12 months, and you need to first complete the five-month eligibility period.

If we can do the five-month eligibility period and then get paid for the full 12 months, that is most advantageous to our clients.

Always discuss the retroactive period with your attorney before filing an application payment.

Tip #52: Representative Payees

In most cases, you will be the only "Payee" if you are awarded benefits.

In some cases, however, if you have difficulty managing your funds and handling money, Social Security will appoint a "Representative Payee" to assist you with managing your funds. Having a Representative Payee means that rather than the checks coming directly to you, they will go to the person you selected as the Representative Payee to manage the funds for you.

It comes into play usually on a mental health claim or a claim when the person is physically incapacitated and unable to make decisions on their own.

A Representative Payee option should always be discussed with your attorney before filing an application. So, Social Security knows who to pay once the case is approved.

It is also possible that the Judge may independently decide to appoint a Representative Payee if he/she feels that you need assistance in handling your benefits each month. If you require a Representative Payee, always make sure that it is someone you trust to handle your money for you.

Tip #53: Easy to Apply

It is now easier than ever to apply for Social Security Disability benefits.

While the Supplemental Security Income application must still be done by the District Office or on paper, the Social Security Disability Insurance program allows you to go to www.ssa.gov[5] and complete the application online. This is not a difficult process and can be easily done if you have the time to do it, which is usually about 30 to 45 minutes.

Alternatively, if you get overwhelmed by forms and questions, or you're just uncertain how to answer some of these complicated questions, you can always call a reputable attorney (or my office,) and we will gladly do the application for you.

Before completing the application, I recommend that you be familiar with your basic information, like your complete legal name, address, phone number, dates of birth, and Social Security number, as well as your diagnosis, symptoms, medications, and treating medical providers.

One of the most important questions on the application is, "When did your disability begin?"

This is called your "Onset Date," and it usually corresponds with when you stopped working — specifically when you stopped earning *Substantial Gainful Activity*.

You must have that Onset Date ready to go as you complete the application, and you must bear in mind that the Onset Date is the starting point of when SSA will pay you if you are approved. Remember that an SSI application will only pay you from the application date forward, while that SSDI application can potentially pay you up to one year before the application date. Having said that, note that even if your Onset Date is more than 12 months before your application date, SSA will only go retroactively one year from the SSDI application date and pay you for those 12 months.

---

5. http://www.ssa.gov

Finally, if you complete the SSDI application online, make sure that you print out and save the online confirmation page that confirms that an application was filed. You may need it at some point in the future in case SSA can't find the application.

Yes, it does happen.

Tip #54: Partnerships

Many people don't realize that the Social Security disability process is a combination of multiple partnerships.

Firstly, there is a partnership between you and your Social Security District Office case manager, who processes a case.

There is also a partnership between you and the Disability Determination Services claims manager, who is responsible for the medical portion of your application, requests the medical records, orders the consultative examinations, and sends you multiple forms to complete.

There is a partnership between you and your physician providing you care.

There is a partnership between you and your attorney representing you on the case.

And there's the partnership between you and yourself.

Let's quickly review how these partnerships work so we can tap into the relationships that will be formed through these partnerships.

As stated above, the first partnership is between you and the Social Security Administration District Office. The Social Security Administration will be the starting point of your journey toward getting benefits. The Social Security Administration is responsible for processing your personal, citizenship, and residency information. It is also responsible for reviewing your credits to see if you qualify for the Social Security Disability Insurance program. That is all the Social Security Administration does. They do not review the medical portion of your case. So if you're finding that Social Security has not initiated your application, and as the process is taking a long time just to get the application into the computer system, you want to reach out to your Social Security case manager, who is your partner in this first part of the process in order to clarify why Social Security is having difficulty processing your case.

The case is then passed to the next partner in the process, the Disability Determination Services.

Your partnership with Disability Determination Services is essential for helping you win your claim. It is the Disability Determination Services that request all of the medical records from your medical providers. The Social Security Disability Determination Services must be provided with a list of all your medical providers, addresses, phone numbers, and fax numbers so that the medical records can be requested. This partnership is very important because if the medical records are not received or obtained by the Disability Determination Services, then a phone call must be made to the case manager to figure out why the medical records were not received. You cannot expect to win your Social Security application and receive a favorable decision Unless you are in touch with your partner at Disability Determination Services.

The next partnership is between you and your doctor.

Your medical providers should be on board and partner with you in this journey for Social Security Disability benefits. Your doctors provide medical notes to the Social Security Administration and Disability Determination Services. You will find, from time to time, that some doctors do not want to participate in the process because they have negative experience doing workers' compensation claims or long-term disability claims. And those are very complex application processes that require multiple forms to be filled out by the physician. With a Social Security Disability case, however, there are no multiple forms that need to be filled out by your physician. Rather, all they need to do is provide the medical records to the Disability Determination Services. If your doctor is unwilling to be your partner in this journey toward obtaining disability benefits, you should consider finding a new doctor. You want your doctor to be a partner in helping you get approved for disability benefits.

The next relationship is between you and your attorney.

I cannot emphasize enough the importance of this partnership. In fact, the purpose of this book you are holding in your hands is to help you understand the Social Security process and how to get approved for benefits. Your attorney is the main strategist in this process and will speak to SSA and the Judge on their behalf. You must have an excellent rapport with your attorney and be in regular contact with him/her to maintain a solid relationship. If you move or change telephone numbers or email addresses, you must ensure that your attorney has all the updated contact information.

The final partnership is between you and yourself.

Applying for Social Security Disability benefits is a long journey, indeed. It requires patience and an understanding of all the different components of the Social Security chronology, as outlined in this book. You need to be committed to going to the doctor. You need to be committed to returning all the Social Security forms. You need to be committed to going into the consultative examinations. And you need to be committed to attending your hearing before the Administrative Law Judge. You cannot quit at any point in the process, or you will lose your claim. Of all the relationships mentioned above, the most important relationship and partnership is the one with yourself. You must be a partner with yourself and commit to yourself that you will do everything it takes in order to win your Social Security case.

Partnerships and understanding the players and their partnership roles are the keys to success in winning a Social Security disability claim.

Tip #55: Keep a Copy of Everything

In this age, when so many items are faxed or mailed to your Social Security District Office or Disability Determination Services offices, you need to keep a record of everything you send in for processing.

Often, I speak to clients who claim that they have filed appeals or submitted information to Social Security, only for Social Security to claim that they have no record of the information submitted to the office.

In some cases, there is a 60-day deadline for submitting an appeal, and we must protectively file that application and have proof that the application was filed promptly.

This does not need to be a long chapter; it can be summed up in a few words; keep a copy of everything.

Medical records, appeals, applications, and any other document sent to Social Security should have a copy in your files at home or with your attorney so that it can be referenced later if you face any problem with your case.

Keep a copy of everything!!!

Tip #56: Never Ever Give Up!

Over the years, I have represented thousands of individuals in their journey to obtain Social Security and disability benefits. Persistence and commitment to the process are the most important ingredients to a successful Social Security claim. All I want to tell you in this chapter is never give up! Never! Give! Up!

People don't realize they have tens of thousands of dollars at stake when applying for Social Security Disability benefits. Understanding the amount of money you have at stake should compel you to stay the course and keep fighting.

The national data shows that 70% of all applications will be denied.

Don't give up. Appeal.

The national data tells us that 85% of all Disability Insurances Reconsiderations are denied.

Don't give up. Appeal.

The national data tells us that the win rates at the hearing are between 45 and 55%, depending on your state if you do not have an attorney. Having an attorney during the hearing will boost your chances of winning up to 75% or 80%.

If your hearing is denied, you still have a chance to get the Judge's decision reversed at the Social Security Appeals Council. Even though only three to 5% of those claims are remanded for a new hearing or are automatically approved, you should still file for an appeal since you have a lot of money at stake.

If the Appeals Council denies your decision, you have your final opportunity to file a claim in Federal District Court. You will need an attorney to assist you with filing your claim in Federal District Court.

The emphasis should be on never ever giving up!

You have five opportunities to win your case. You have to keep fighting to move the case along.

It is especially true when you don't feel good mentally or physically.

There will be days when you feel terrible and cannot get out of bed.

Don't forget that if you are feeling overwhelmed by the long and arduous process, it is okay to give yourself a little tender loving care and take a break or a few days off from working on your case or allow your attorney to take the lead. We all need to catch our breath from time-to-time.

Nevertheless, you should never give up or get frustrated by the process's length or difficulty.

Tip #57: Mental Conditions Can be Disabling

There are a lot of uninformed people who think that disability benefits are only based on physical disabilities.

Many people don't realize that mental health impairments are also disabling. Mental health impairments are called the "invisible disease" since, in most cases, you cannot "see" the mental impairment in the same way you can see a physical impairment.

Whether your mental health claim is based on Schizophrenia, Bipolar, Major Depressive Disorder, General Anxiety Disorder, Post-Traumatic Stress Disorder, or any other mental impairment, you should know that Social Security regulations guide and navigate us toward getting a mental health case approved.

As mentioned earlier in this book, the Social Security Administration have determined what they expected to see in the medical records to get an impairment approved. The Social Security Adult Disability Listings, Section 12.0, deals with mental health listings and can be found online at www.ssa.gov[6]. If you google "SSA listings and 12.0," the Social Security mental health listings will appear in your search results. You can click those search results and review all Social Security mental health listings in the 12.0 section. I highly recommend that you do this.

I have six tips for winning a mental health claim:

1. You must go to a doctor to care for your mental health impairment every month for at least a year;
2. The doctor must make those notes available to Social Security so that they can review your mental health limitations and restrictions;
3. There can be no current drugs and alcohol on your records;
4. You must be under a prescribed medication regimen by your doctor and in compliance with that medication regimen;
5. You should get a non-exertional Residual functional capacity

---

6. http://www.ssa.gov

questionnaire completed by your mental health professional, which outlines your mental limits and restrictions;

6. Lastly, and I cannot emphasize this enough, get an experienced attorney to help you with your claim for benefits.

Presenting a case to a Judge is similar to an artist taking out their canvass, brushes and paints, and then painting a picture. You and your attorney need to paint a picture to the Judge of what it is like to be YOU every single day of the week. You need to add details and colors to your limitations and restrictions, especially when it comes to mental health impairments which are more difficult to establish.

Tip #58: Emergency Contacts

I cannot emphasize enough on the importance of staying in touch with your attorney and the Social Security Administration.

You think that this is a basic requirement that should be self-explanatory to everyone. Believe me, it is not.

At least once a week, I have a client who calls me out of the blue and tells me that they moved and changed their contact number and email address. It is essential that you keep your attorney and Social Security advised of any changes in your contact information.

For that reason, I always collect emergency contact numbers for my clients. Why? Because, believe it or not, they keep going missing or disappearing on me in the middle of the process.

Having the name of a friend or a family member on hand in case you disappear can make all the difference between winning and losing a case. Without emergency contacts, if you disappear, Social Security and your attorney have no way of finding you or contacting you, and you will probably lose your claim.

Always make sure that emergency contact, telephone numbers, and other information are provided to the Social Security Administration or your attorney.

It is also a good idea to let your emergency contacts know that you have put their names down with your attorney as emergency contacts in case the attorney ever needs to reach out to them to find you. Please don't get lost or disappear on your attorney.

Tip #59: Retirement Benefits Versus Disability Benefits

Many people ask me if they can collect retirement benefits at the same time that they collect disability Insurance (SSDI) benefits. The answer never varies, for it is always *no*

You cannot double-dip. You can either collect retirement benefits OR disability benefits. Not both.

So how do you choose which benefits you should take? The retirement benefits or the disability benefits?

The answer is that you need to know your benefit amount for the retirement benefits, and you need to know the benefit amount for the disability benefits, and then do the calculations to see which benefits works for you.

The best way to determine the benefit amount is to call your local Social Security District Office and tell them that you are unsure if you want to collect disability or retirement benefits. Remember, retirement benefits are on a sliding scale based on your retirement age. So, if you take retirement benefits early, you may not get the full retirement amount that you would get if you waited until full retirement age.

So, what you want to do is you want to determine the age that you want to retire, and then call your local Social Security Disability Office and ask them simply how much will my benefit amount if you take disability benefits versus how much will my benefit amount be if you take retirement benefits at your early age. It is the only way you'll be able to tell what makes the most sense for you.

SSI is different; you can collect both Retirement benefits and SSI benefits at the same time. Once again, I recommend that you call your local SSA District Office for more information on this option.

In conclusion, you cannot collect both retirement benefits and disability insurance benefits.

It's either one or the other.

The best way to select the right option is to call your local Social Security District Office and match the numbers up one against the other.

Tip #60: Disability Benefits Are Taxable

Everyone hates to pay taxes. I don't care who you are; no one likes to pay taxes. Unfortunately, your Social Security disability benefits may be taxed depending if you're single or married.

If you are single and receive over $25,000 in the course of a year, those benefits will be taxed.

For a married couple, if you receive over $32,000 a year, those benefits will be taxed.

Since this book specializes in tips and advice relating to winning your disability benefits, we are going to keep the focus on the purpose of this book which is to help you win your disability case.

As such, you should consult a competent accountant or financial service agency to determine if you need to pay taxes on your disability benefits.

Tip # 61: Don't Take a Vacation

We all like to get away every now and then with our friends and families. Many of us look forward to time away so that we can recharge our batteries.

At your hearing, the Administrative Law Judges will often ask if you have taken any vacations in the last year or two or since you filed for your application?

It is a tricky question at the hearing since many people will simply answer yes or no, and the Judge will ask them where they went, and they will tell the Judge about their vacation destination. Thus, they don't understand what's the reason behind such questions.

In reality, the Judge is trying to figure out your capacity and capabilities to travel and engage in multiple activities during a vacation.

How far did you drive in the car question? How long were you able to sit? Did you take an airplane? How did you handle your luggage? Did you go swimming? Did you go hiking? Did you perform any other activities that made Judges doubt if you are disabled or not?

I am not saying that you cannot take a vacation. But, my recommendation for people who need to be accompanied when they take a vacation is that they let the Judge know that they were able to take a vacation and needed assistance through every step of the process.

From the driving to the lifting, the luggage, the transportation, and the activities, they needed assistance, and their recovery time was extensive. They also need to inform the Judge if they need to be heavily medicated when traveling. Due to anxiety or pain, there are some people who need medication when they are traveling.

Always be on guard and aware of what the Judge is asking when they ask questions that seem basic and simple. If at all possible, it is best not to take vacations when your application is pending, as that may negatively reflect your ability to engage in basic activities.

If by chance, you did take a vacation, you should let the Judge know. But, you should also let the Judge know the difficulties you had while travelling (i.e. you couldn't sit for long, you need a wheelchair transport at the airport, you required the use of an attendant at all times, etc). You do NOT want to give an impression to the Judge that you were scuba diving or playing volleyball on the beach. You do NOT want to give an impression to the Judge that you were able to easily transport yourself to another far-away destination without any difficulty. If not handled correctly, it can blow-up your entire claim.

Tip # 62: Social Media

Is Social Security Administration surfing your Instagram account to see if you're performing and posting pictures or if you are engaged in your activities? Is the Social Security Administration reviewing your Facebook accounts to see what pictures you post? Is the Social Security Administration inspecting your Tik Tok account or other social media accounts? That is the million-dollar question.

In theory, the answer should or could be — yes.

The Cooperative Disability Investigations (CDI) program is a key anti-fraud initiative that combats fraud within Social Security disability programs. The CDI program accomplishes its mission by reviewing questionable disability claims and investigating cases of suspected disability fraud in order to stop payment before it occurs or as soon as fraud is suspected.

Each CDI unit consists of a Social Security Administration (SSA) Office of the Inspector General (OIG) special agent who serves as a team leader, personnel from SSA, State Disability Determination Services (DDS), and State or local law enforcement partners. CDI units combine federal and state resources and expertise to benefit not only Social Security programs but also other federal and state programs, such as food and nutrition assistance, housing assistance, Medicare, and Medicaid.

No one knows exactly how many people are working in this department or what investigatory tactics and techniques they use to determine if someone is engaged in fraud. So, in theory, it is possible that they're surfing your social media accounts to see what activities you post and if, in fact, you are truly not disabled.

However, in actuality, I highly doubt they are surfing the internet and looking at your social media pages, unless someone has reported you to SSA. There are millions of SSA beneficiaries. It is so difficult to just get Social Security to allocate employees to process applications, process appeals, collect medical records, and do other required items to get approved on a disability claim, let alone have them surf the internet for your social media pictures.

There are barely enough employees to do every aspect required to win a case. Every department is short-staffed during COVID times; many offices have their staff working remotely, and the process already takes much longer than it should. To go ahead and make the leap and jump that they are taking the time to surf your social media accounts seems excessive, unless you believe that someone had a reason to report you.

I personally believe that the OIG _does_ investigate suspicious activity and that I usually reserve that opinion for investigations relating to money earned while collecting disability benefits. Remember, you're not allowed to earn over SGA when you are applying for disability benefits or collecting disability benefits.

In conclusion, while the SSA department and the OIG may be reviewing your social media accounts, it is highly unlikely they will pick your account to review, unless someone has reported you. Nevertheless, you should refrain from posting pictures of you engaged in activities that may call your disability into suspicion.

Tip #63: Say Thank You

When was the last time you said "thank you" to your caretaker, loved one, or friend who has been assisting you while you are unable to care for yourself.

While this book is focused on tips and advice on how to win your claim for disability benefits, it is worthwhile to take a moment and remind every reader to say "Thank you" to your caretakers.

After all, they help you get out of bed, get dressed, shower, and/or bathe, as well as help you with food shopping and preparing meals.

In many cases, they may be assisting you by driving you to and from doctor appointments or other medical appointments that you have to attend.

Don't they deserve a sincere and genuine *Thank you*?

Yes, they do. They need to hear from you how much you truly appreciate their help at this difficult time in your life.

Go to the store and buy them a "Thank You" card – they deserve it!

They have been there for you. You need to say Thank You.

Tip #64: Good Cause Letters

As we've discussed many times before, 70% of all disability applications will get denied.

When you receive your denial letter, it will state to you how to file an appeal. You can do it online, you can fax it in, or you can submit it by paper and in person at a local SSA District Office. Alternatively, if you are totally confused about how to do it, you can call your local SSA District Office and get a protective filing date for your appeal over the telephone, showing that it was filed timely.

But what I want to focus on in this chapter is something called a "good cause" letter.

As you may already know, when your claim gets denied, you have 60 calendar days to submit your appeal for Reconsideration or your Request for a Hearing. There are many people who don't know how to do this. The easiest way is to do it online at www.ssa.gov[7] or go on the Internet and download the form and fax it to your local SSA District office. When you do it online, you're able to print out the confirmation that your appeal was received, and you should keep it for your records. When you fax in your appeal, you should keep a copy of the fax confirmation letter showing that it was sent successfully.

But what happens if you don't file your appeal within 60 days?

In almost all cases, the SSA District Office will not process your appeal, as it was not filed timely.

There is one exception to this rule of not filing within 60 days of the denial date. That exception is if you have a "good cause" reason for why you did not file your appeal timely.

---

7. http://www.ssa.gov

Perhaps you were in the hospital? Perhaps you didn't understand your rights? Perhaps your mailbox keeps getting broken into, and you're not receiving your mail, and you did not receive the denial letter? Maybe the SSA notice was in a language you couldn't understand? There are a host of good cause reasons why you didn't submit your appeal within the 60-day time limit.

What you need to do is draft a good cause letter to your local SSA District and provide a good cause reason why you did not submit your appeal timely within the 60-day requirement. You must clearly state your reasons and your good causes and submit any other documentation that may support this reason showing why you couldn't file your appeal timely (i.e., you were in the hospital, and you have a copy of your discharge report).

You are going to need to follow up on your good-cause late filing, so make sure that you call your local SSA District Office a few days after filing your good-cause reason for the late filing to confirm that they received this request.

It should be noted that it is not enough to just file the letter.

You must also attach the proper Request for Reconsideration form or the Request for Hearing before an Administrative Law Judge form with your good cause letter in order to make sure that everything is processed correctly.

Ideally, you should have an attorney assist you with this process as it can become a little overwhelming for a novice or for someone who has no experience in drafting good-cause letters. A skilled, qualified, and experienced attorney knows how to successfully draft and submit a good cause letter for late filing.

As I've done so many times before in this book, I highly recommend that you hire an attorney to assist you with this and other aspects of your case. I cannot emphasize enough on the important role that an attorney will play in saving your case if you don't file within the 60-day timeframe for appealing your denied claim.

My tip for this chapter is don't let your appeal go down the toilet just because you didn't file timely. You MUST find a good cause reason why you didn't file timely, even if it is because you didn't understand how to file the appeal, and you should submit that good cause reason to your local SSA District Office.

Remember, you have a lot of money at stake, and you don't want to start from the beginning. At all costs, try to save your case with a good cause late filing letter.

Tip #65: Good Attorney Versus Bad Attorney

There are many different types of attorneys that you can hire to assist you with your claim for benefits. In short, there are good attorneys, there are bad attorneys, and there are great attorneys.

A bad attorney is an attorney who just takes your case and does very little work on your case toward a successful resolution. They may file the application or appeal and sit on it for many months, not taking any action to move the case forward. Some attorneys barely even read the medical records before a hearing, and at the hearing, they say very little to the Judge or to advocate on your behalf at the hearing. I've seen it happen.

A good attorney will play an active role in every aspect of your case.

The attorney will be in touch with you regularly.

The attorney is available by email or telephone to discuss and strategize your case.

The attorney is on top of the medical record requests.

The attorney has reviewed the medical records before the hearing, and the attorney takes an active role in advocating for your case at the time of the hearing.

A great attorney has one extra quality, and that quality is being passionate.

You should find a great attorney who is passionate about their work and your case.

After all, that passion will engage the attorney, that extra amount to fight for your case toward a successful resolution.

A good attorney knows how to present the case, and a great attorney knows how to win a case.

A great attorney will always be by your side during every aspect of the case to answer your questions, hold your hand, encourage you, and advocate on your behalf, either at the District Office, the Disability Determination Services office, or at the hearing with the Judge.

Always try to find an attorney with that extra passion and select that attorney to represent you in the case.

Tip #66: Never, Never, Never

There are a bunch of Nevers that should be included in our conversation regarding hearings with a Judge.

Never lie to the Judge.

Never Joke around with the Judge.

Never lose your patience with the Judge.

Never interrupt a Judge or talk over the Judge.

Never argue with the Judge.

Never insult the intelligence of the Judge.

More than anything else, Judges like to control their courts and the direction of their hearings. The courtroom is their little kingdom, and they like to have control over the hearing as it takes place. They hate it when the Claimant interrupts them. They hate it when the Claimant argues with them. And more than anything else, they will know if you are lying to the Judge.

I cannot emphasize enough the importance of having respect for the court by being honest and patient as your hearing progresses.

Never, never, never break the above rules.

Tip #67: All the Facts

Many Claimants don't realize that during the hearing process, it is their opportunity to present ALL of the evidence into the record that they are disabled.

In fact, the hearing is considered a fact-finding process where the Judge makes many inquiries into the exhibits and testimony in order to determine all the facts of the case. It is very important to get <u>all</u> the facts **"on the record"** at the time of or before the hearing.

This is especially important because if your hearing is denied and you decide to appeal your case to the Social Security Appeals Council, the Appeals Council will not be a new fact-finder.

There is no fact-finding at the Appeals Council level. All the Appeals Council generally looks for is if there was an "error of law" made by the Judge. It is very difficult to introduce new evidence into the record at the Appeals Council.

All fact-finding must occur "on the record" at the hearing in order for it to be part of the official record and considered by the Judge. You cannot present more evidence once the decision is written.

It must all be presented either prior to or at the hearing. Or, prior to the decision being signed by the Judge.

Tip #68: Supplemental Hearings

It is important to try to wrap up the complete hearing experience with the Judge at the time of the first, and hopefully only, disability hearing.

However, there are many examples of why a second or supplemental hearing may be required. If additional evidence is presented into the record post-hearing, the Judge may decide to hold a supplemental or second hearing in order to inquire about the new evidence.

Additionally, after reviewing the medical evidence in the file, the Judge may decide to call a supplemental hearing if they wish to get the testimony of a Medical Expert or a Vocational Expert who is specialized in jobs.

A medical and Vocational Expert is not always 100% guaranteed to be part of the first hearing.

Often, the Judge may request for these experts to appear at a supplemental hearing if the Judge needs additional information relating to either the medical evidence or the past relevant work or if there are any other jobs in the national economy that the Claimant can do.

A supplemental hearing may be required after your first hearing if the Judge cannot make a conclusion and a decision at the time of the first hearing.

Tip #69: Submitting Evidence Until the Decision

Suppose you have your hearing, submitted all of your medical evidence to the Judge at the time of the hearing, and then go off the record. You "closed the record" for the Judge to make the decision on your case, and thereafter, before you receive your written decision, you end up having a new medical exam or emergency after the hearing that the Judge needs to know about as part of your case.

Many people are unaware that they can submit any new evidence they want up until the time of the decision. However, once the decision is written, it becomes difficult to submit new facts or evidence to the record.

I recommend that everybody stay in touch with their attorney and be aware that if <u>any</u> new medical issues arise <u>after</u> the hearing, they let their attorney know that these new medical documents be submitted to the Judge and into the record before the decision is made.

More often than you would believe, Claimants have their hearings, and while they are waiting for the decision from the Judge, they end up in the hospital. Yes, those new post-hearing records need to be submitted to the Judge.

You must always include a cover letter explaining why the new post-hearing records are material to the case, but once you do you can always submit new evidence to the record before the Judge decides the case.

Tip #70: Five-Day Letter

While new evidence can always be submitted into the record, many Judges will reject any new evidence submitted within five days of the hearing unless there are extenuating circumstances why the medical records weren't submitted before five days.

It is called the 'five-day letter rule.'

Anytime you submit new evidence to the record within five days of the hearing, it must be accompanied by a 'five-day' letter.

Sometimes some medical providers utilize a copy service to help them produce medical records. These copy services move very slowly. Sometimes they will not produce the medical records in time for the hearing. It is not uncommon for a copy service to take even 60 to 90 to 120 days to produce the records.

If there is a delay in obtaining medical records and those medical records need to be submitted within five days of the hearing, or if there are extenuating circumstances outside of the control of the Claimant of the attorney as to why the new evidence was not submitted within five days, a five-day letter must be accompanied with the new medical evidence, explaining the circumstances so that the evidence can be submitted into the record.

When did you request the records? How did you request them? What is the delay? The Judge wants the answers to these questions in the five-day letter.

The five-day letter is not a suggestion. It is not a recommendation. It is not optional. It is mandatory.

Tip #71: Staying in Touch With Your Attorney

Earlier in this book, we spoke about the importance of updating your attorney with any new telephone numbers or addresses or email addresses so that your attorney can stay in touch with you. Again, I've included this chapter because it isn't just about the attorney having your updated information. Rather, It's about staying in touch with your attorney and regularly bring the attorney up to date on any aspects of the case you feel the attorney should be aware of.

Maybe you have recently been approved for In-Home Health Services, or have recently been prescribed a new assistive device. Perhaps you had to take a trip to the Emergency Room or were admitted to the hospital... does your attorney know?

If you complete a Function Report or a Work History report or if you attend a Consultative Examination, or even if Social Security calls you on the telephone to discuss your case with you, you should be in touch with your attorney and bring your attorney up to date as to the new events that occurred on your case.

You want your attorney to know you by your first name and be familiar with your case. Some Claimants never call their attorney; as a result, their file is left untouched for many months. In contrast, other clients, who call the attorney every few weeks to discuss the case, will always have an attorney who is up-to-date on their case.

Always stay in touch with your attorney, up to the point that the attorney knows you on a first-name basis.

Tip #72: In It to Win It

I like to say that your attorney should be "in it to win it."

It means that any hurdle, any challenges, any obstacles, or any roadblocks that come in the way between you and your decision will be overcome by your attorney because your attorney is "in it to win it."

You shouldn't be just a file number in the attorney's office. You are a person who is disabled, and this is your life we are talking about!

Some attorneys are very particular and even superstitious about how to win a case. They don't put their faith in the merits of the medical records, but rather depend on superstitions and other omens

For instance, they want that the hearing be assigned to a certain hearing office in order to win the case. Or, if the Judge has a low approval rating, they try to get assigned to another Judge. Or, the hearing needs to be assigned on a certain day of the week in order to win the case.

This is all nonsense and rubbish.

Nothing should stop your attorney from trying to win your case, if your attorney is "in it to win it." Your attorney has to be ready to enter that hearing "full speed ahead."

My strongest advice, is to not just select an attorney because they showed up high on your google rankings. Read the reviews. Get a sense of what type of attorney you are hiring. Bottom line, is your attorney "in it to win it" or not? That is the question.

Tip #73: Medications

You'd be surprised, but many people are unaware of the names of the medications that they're taking. They are clueless when it comes to dosage amounts.

More surprisingly, many people are even unaware of *why* they're taking the medications in the first place.

It becomes a real problem when attending the Consultative Examination with the Department of Disability Determination Services, and at the hearing with the Judge.

You need to know the name of the medications you're taking. You need to know the dosage amount. You need to know why you're taking the medications, and you need to know the side effects of those medications.

This is especially important when you attend your Consultative Examination. Write the names of the medications down on a piece of paper and put the paper in your wallet or pocketbook so that you have the list readily available when asked about your medications.

Side effects of medications can play a big role at the hearing.

Do you get tired from the medications? Do you get nauseous or dizzy from the medications? Do the medications result in a change of appetite or loss of weight? Is there a change to your bathroom habits?

The multiple side effects become apparent very quickly once you present what medications you are taking, the medications' role, and the strength of the medications. Make sure at the hearing that you get all of your medications on the record before the Judge. A medication form should be completed before the hearing so the Judge can submit this medication form as part of the evidence in the record.

In the movie Marry Poppins, there is a song that says just a spoonful of sugar helps the medicine go down.

I'd like to change that: just the spoonful of knowledge helps the medicine go down.

Always provide SSA and the Judge with the most updated list of your medications. It is relevant.

You must be knowledgeable about your medications, so the Judge can know what role the medications play in deciding your disability.

Tip #74: Who Did You Speak To?

Often, we call the Social Security Administration or Disability Determination Services, or the Office of Hearings and Operations, and we have someone that assists us on the telephone.

You must get the name, telephone number, and/or extension of the person who is helping you.

You should notate the name of the person who helped you with your request.

It sometimes happens that many months later, there may have been an error in processing your case, and you need to be able to write a letter to the District Office or the Judge explaining the situation and who it was in that office who helped you.

The District Offices and the hearing offices are familiar with their staff, as well as the staff names, and if they can track down who you spoke with and what your request was, then they will often give you more leeway in helping push the matter forward when the time comes to push the matter forward.

Always know who you spoke with and make a note of it so you can reference it later if you need it.

Tip #75: Are You A Student?

Many years ago, the traditional school required students to attend classes in person at the campus where the courses were delivered. The student had to drive a car or take public transportation to school. The student had to carry their book bag to the classes, remain seated in a classroom, take notes, and take a full curriculum of classes and credits during a semester.

Nowadays, we live in amazing times.

Everything can be done online, especially in a post-COVID world. Almost all schools offer online classes which allow you to take a class from the comfort of your home.

You no longer need to drive the campus, carry your heavy book bags, walk across campus to the classroom and exert yourself in the same way you used to do years ago when you had to attend classes live and in person.

Therefore, I don't see any reason why you cannot attend a school or continue your education when your application or your appeal is pending with the Social Security Administration. It is worthwhile to note that in the conversation of substantial gainful activity, attending school used to be considered under the definition of substantial gainful activity, but for the reasons mentioned above, that is really no longer the case.

New applicants who are attending classes at or part of a special disability program that is offered for disabled students can now take comfort in knowing that they can attend their classes online. It should not affect their application or appeal.

Tip #76: Who Decides If You Should Apply?

As a disability attorney and practicing for the last 25 years, the question I am asked the most is "should I apply for disability benefits?"

Unfortunately, I am the wrong person to answer that question.

You should never let the attorney decide whether or not you are a good candidate for disability benefits.

The person who should decide if you're eligible for disability benefits is your doctor.

It is your doctor who understands your medical conditions and the restrictions and limitations which you may have because of your impairments. I recommend that you have a conversation with three different parties before deciding whether to file disability benefits or not.

The first person you should have a conversation with is your doctor. As mentioned above, the doctor is familiar with and has the expertise to determine if you are disabled or not. It is also important to have your doctor's support since your doctor will need to provide documentation to the Social Security Administration to determine if you are disabled or not. You want to have your doctor as a partner in this process. So, I highly recommend that you speak to your doctor before deciding whether or not to apply for disability benefits.

The next party to speak would be your family and support group.

Applying for disability benefits can take up to two years, and you will need to have the support of your family and support group during this time. Whether you require assistance financially, physically, or emotionally, it is your family and support group who will be providing you with the assistance you need during this waiting period of two years. You want to make sure that your family is on board and able to help you during this time. They need to understand that this is a long process and that you will be looking to them for support during this period.

Finally, after speaking to your doctor and your family, friends, family, and friends, the person you should have a conversation with as to whether or not you should apply for disability benefits is yourself.

You need to be committed to this process; you need to understand that this is a two-year process. You need to strengthen yourself to understand that you are the one who needs to go for the examinations, the laboratory work, as well as any other procedures that may be required in order for you to qualify for disability benefits. Often, many Claimants give up halfway through the journey to acquire their disability benefits because it's taking too long or because it's too typical of a process. For that reason, I highly recommend that you have a conversation with yourself to see if you are up to the challenge.

The decision to apply for disability benefits should never be made by the attorney. The attorney should only be consulted <u>after</u> first speaking to your doctor, your family and support group, and yourself.

Tip # 77: Active Work Credits

In general, a Claimant must earn 40 Social Security credits to qualify for Social Security Disability Insurance benefits.

Each time you work "on the books," you earn credits.

The number of credits does not affect the amount of benefits you receive. The credits only determine your eligibility for disability benefits. SSA will not pay benefits to you if you don't have enough credits.

Since 1978, you earn up to a maximum of four credits per year which are based on your total wages and self-employment income for the year. You might work all year to earn four credits, or you might earn enough for all four in much less time.

The amount of earnings it takes to earn a credit may change each year.

In 2023, you earn one Social Security or Medicare credit for every $1,640 in covered earnings each year. You must earn $6,560 to get the maximum four credits for the year. Does that make sense? It should.

The SSA web page states that during your lifetime, you might earn more credits than the minimum number you need to be eligible for benefits. These extra credits do not increase your benefit amount. The average of your earnings over your working years, not the total number of credits you earn, determines how much your monthly payment will be when you receive benefits.

If you are self-employed, you earn Social Security credits the same way employees do (1 credit for each $1,640 in net earnings, but no more than 4 credits per year).If you are in the military, you earn Social Security credits the same way civilian employees do.

The number of credits necessary to meet the recent work test depends on your age.

The rules are as follows:

- **Before age 24** — You may qualify if you have 6 credits earned in the 3-year period ending when your disability starts.

- **Age 24 to 31** — In general, you may qualify if you have credit for working half the time between age 21 and the time your disability began. As a general example, if you develop a disability at age 27, you would need 3 years of work (12 credits) out of the past 6 years (between ages 21 and 27).

- **Age 31 or older** — In general, you must have at least 20 credits in the 10-year period immediately before your disability begins.

Developed a disability at age	Credits needed	Years of work
31 through 42	20	5
44	22	5 ½
46	24	6
48	26	6 ½
50	28	7
52	30	7 ½
54	32	8
56	34	8 ½
58	36	9
60	38	9 ½
62 or older	40	10

Tip # 78: Say "Cheese"

WHO REMEMBERS WHEN they were younger, and they had to take the class picture at school?

The photographer would line you up in front of the camera and then see the magic words "Say cheese!"

That was your signal to smile for the camera.

I am regularly asked by my clients if they can submit pictures of themselves to the Judge or videos of themselves to the Judge before the hearing.

I can tell you, after representing thousands of individuals before hearings Judges, that I have never seen a Judge admit a video of the person talking or demonstrating the restrictions and limitations by video. They just don't do it. It doesn't happen.

But what about pictures?

Can I show a picture of my swollen legs? What about the rash on my skin? What about the size of the hernia on my abdomen? What about my open wound? Will the Judge accept a picture?

The answer to this question is difficult to answer, and it really depends on a Judge-by-Judge basis.

I have seen some Judges accept images and pictures, and I've seen other Judges who will not accept images and pictures as they feel and embrace the concept of "justice is blind" and that they should solely base their decisions on medical records.

Here is what I do.

I drafted a cover letter to the Judge, explaining that I am submitting to the record several images that I want to be considered at the hearing, and I attached the pictures.

Before the Judge can even decide whether or not to admit this image as a picture, he or she has *already viewed the pictures!* It's too late. The damage is done.

The Judge has seen with his or her own eyes the extent of the medical impairment and will not be able to get the image out of their head.

They are in a jam.

And, in most cases, as the saying goes, a picture says 1000 words.

I recently had a case of a lady who had a hernia in her abdomen region. The hernia was the size of a small basketball. It was clear that once you saw a picture of the hernia on the Claimant, there was no way she could walk, bend, stoop, crouch, or crawl. She really won the case based on the picture. No amount of medical records could adequately explain the extent or the severity of the hernia in the way that the picture could. Using the approach above, I submitted the picture and then argued with the Judge about the materiality and relevance of the picture, and even though the picture was not admitted into the record, she still won her case.

In my heart, I believe that she won her case because the Judge saw the picture, even though it wasn't admitted as evidence, and knew that the case had to be approved.

I had a similar situation when I recently had a hearing before a Judge where the Claimant had severely swollen feet, legs, and ankles. They were not only big and puffy but were also red and shiny.

She took a picture of her foot next to a shoe, and it was clear that there was no way that she could put on the shoe.

The Judge admitted the picture to the record, and I referenced the picture in the hearing when the time came to question the Claimant about their ability to ambulate and their ability to wear shoes. Once again, as I said above, a picture says 1000 words.

While Judges do not like to receive pictures or images, if you have a medical impairment that is visible to the naked eye, I would nevertheless submit a picture of it next to your DMV driver's license. After all, the Judge needs to use your driver's license to establish your identity and confirm that you are the person in fact in the picture.

Listen... Do you want to win this case or not? Of course, you do!

Having said that, you should be employing every technique possible in order to prove your case to the Judge. Submitting a picture or image next to your identification is yet another technique for getting your case approved, even if the image or picture is not ultimately submitted into the record.

If you're going to submit a picture, don't forget to say "cheese." ☺

Tip # 79: Attorney Fees

Like anything else in life, if you win your case, you're going to have to pay your attorney for the services provided to win your case.

It should be noted that almost every attorney does not charge you unless you win your case.

So, the only time a fee discussion arises is when a case is approved.

Effective from December 1st, 2022, the Social Security commissioner has stated that an attorney can charge up to 25%, or $7,200, whichever is less, for services rendered.

For many years, this level has been capped at $6,000, but effective December 1, 2022, the Social Security Commission has escalated the $6,000 amount to $7,200. You can rest assured knowing that you will never have to pay more than $7,200 on a regular standard case before a Judge.

The only time that attorney fees vary is when a fee petition is required for either a selected amount of work or for additional work that as put into a case.

A fee petition can occur in two situations. The first situation is when you had another attorney on the case prior to being signed up with your new attorney, and that first attorney is charging you a fee for the services they rendered during the time that they were your attorneys. It means that if the Judge awards $7,200, the first attorney may get $1,200 for the work that they provided. And the other attorney may get $5,000.

How does the Judge determine how much money is allocated to each attorney? Well, each attorney has to submit a fee petition, which is an outline of the hours and services provided, and the amount of time worked on that case. The Judge will then review the hours and services provided and allocate a dollar amount to the first attorney for the work provided and then allocate a second dollar amount to the second attorney for the work provided.

The other situation when a fee petition arises is if the case goes past the Administrative Law Judge level and makes its way all the way to SSA Appeals Counsel or Federal District courts. In that scenario, the attorney can provide an itemized list of services provided and an hourly fee and request that the Judge make an award greater than $7,200 since there was an extensive amount of work put into the case. Once again, you are protected as the Social Security commissioner must approve these fees before the claim can be made to the attorney.

In almost all cases, the attorney fees will either be 25% of the first check, not more than $7,200. Or, if a fee petition is required, it may be more than $7,200 if your case goes to SSA Appeals Counsel or the Federal District court.

Tip #80: Theory of the Case

At one point or another, you may find yourself before a disability Administrative Law Judge who is going to review all aspects of your case and decide if the case should be favorably approved or denied.

You really should not go into this hearing without the help of an attorney, as you have a lot of money at stake, and you're at risk of not being approved for your benefits if your case is not approved at the hearing level.

If you still, however, decide that you do not want to take my advice and you insist on doing the hearing by yourself, you need to make sure that you have a "theory of the case" to present to the Judge.

What do I mean by "theory of the case?"

What I mean is that you cannot just go before the Judge and tell the Judge that you want to be approved for benefits because you "don't feel well," or because "your body hurts," or because you have "a lot of medical conditions." Hello! The Judge already knows that!

You need to present to the Judge a "theory of the case" as to why the application for benefits should be approved. A theory of the case is usually based on the Social Security Adult Listings and/or the Social Security "grid" rules. See the Appendixes at the back of the book for a lengthier description of what Listings and Grid rules are and how to use them.

If you don't understand what the Social Security adult listings are or how to use the grid rules, you will never be able to successfully craft a theory of a case that will be successful in getting you approved.

The Judge is going to look at your age, your education level, as well as your medical diagnosis. But that's not enough! You must have a concrete and focused theory of the case so that the Judge has a pathway to approve your case.

I'm going to give you an example.

Let's say that you have diabetes with neuropathy, asthma, COPD, and depression, as well as anxiety.

As such, after consulting Social Security adult listings, what you would tell the Judge is that the theory of your case, and why your case should be approved, is based on Social Security disability rulings listings 9.0 for diabetes, listing 11.14 for neuropathy, listing 3.03 for asthma, listing 3.02 for COPD, listing 12.04 for depression and listing 12.06 for the anxiety.

Alternatively, if you are 55 or older, and you were not able to stand for more than two hours in a day, you may say that because you have a high school diploma and your past relevant work is unskilled that you meet grid ruling 201.04. Now I know that all that sounds like gibberish to you, but to a trained attorney and a knowledgeable Administrative Law Judge, you have just prepared and presented a well-focused theory of the case.

I will give you another example.

Let's assume that you have fibromyalgia, headaches, anxiety, rheumatoid arthritis, and lupus. Again, you need to have a theory of a case as to why your claim should be approved.

As such, in your opening statement to the Judge, you would state, "Your Honor, the theory of my case, and why my case should be approved is based on the Fibromyalgia Social Security Ruling 12-2p, Social Security Ruling for headaches 19-4p, 12.06 listing for anxiety, rheumatoid arthritis listing 14.06, and lupus listing 14.02." Using your age, education and residual functional exertional capacity level, you may also cite to a grid rule. That is a theory of the case!

Why? Because you're clearly telling the Judge your roadmap for why the Judge should approve your case.

I know all of the above is very confusing and overwhelming for most of you.

I know that most of the above probably did not make sense to most of you.

And that is why I keep emphasizing to all of you that you need to hire an experienced attorney to assist you before the Judge in order to win your claim for benefits.

An experienced and educated disability attorney will know how to present a theory of the case in the opening or closing statements to the Judge.

Once again, it is not enough to just state that you don't feel well, or that your body hurts, or that you have mental problems. Those are descriptions and symptoms. They are not a theory of the case.

My tip, and this is an important one, is to always make sure when you are before a Judge that you have a clear theory of a case that presents a pathway for the Judge to grant you a favorable finding on your claim for benefits

In my opinion, if you've never had a disability hearing before a Judge, you really don't want to mess up your case, and you should be hiring a disability attorney to help you win.

Understanding the importance of a theory of a case shows that you have insight and knowledge of the Social Security process and that you are familiar with the rulings, listings and regulations, and are prepared to present your case to the Judge with all of the necessary evidence in the file to establish your theory of the case.

I would never steer you wrong.

Trust me when I tell you that you should really be hiring an attorney to assist you with your hearing before the Judge at all costs. They will know how to cultivate a compelling theory of the case.

Tip #81: Substantial Gainful Activity

To be eligible for disability benefits, a person must be unable to engage in Substantial Gainful Activity (SGA), for a period of not less than 12 months.

A person who is earning more than a certain monthly amount (net of impairment-related work expenses) is ordinarily considered to be engaging in SGA.

The amount of monthly earnings considered as SGA depends on the nature of a person's disability. The Social Security Act specifies a higher SGA amount for statutorily blind individuals.

The monthly SGA amount for statutorily blind individuals for 2023 is $2,460, and for non-blind individuals, the monthly SGA amount for 2023 is $1,470.

The Social Security regulations do not use the word "work." In the body of the regulations, the rules use the term "Substantial Gainful Activity."

How do we define the word "*substantial*?"

Substantial is defined as significant physical or mental activities you would ordinarily be paid for. If you're engaged in an important physical or mental activity, that will be considered substantial.

How do we define "*gainful*?"

Gainful design is defined as something which you get paid for. If you're doing the type of work you would ordinarily be paying for, then it is considered gainful.

Your work needs to be substantial and gainful before it can be regarded as Substantial Gainful Activity.

Volunteer work should also be considered, as the Judges will look carefully to see if it was substantial volunteer work. Additionally, they will look to see if they volunteer work gainful.

Volunteer work, by its nature, is not paid; it doesn't match up to the gainful activity.

However, if it is the type of work someone has ordinarily paid for because there's a significant amount of physical or mental activity involved in this volunteer work, the Judges may view your volunteer work as substantial and deny disability benefits.

You must be very careful during the application period about what type of volunteer work you do because it may disqualify you because of the Substantial Gainful Activity rules.

Tip #82: Exertional Levels

Vocational exertional levels are as follows: Sedentary, Light, Medium, Heavy, and Very Heavy.

Sedentary work is the type of work that's done; usually, sitting at a desk for a long time requires carrying less than five pounds. It is the typical work done at a desk by a sedentary employee.

The light exertional level is anything between five to 20 pounds. It may include someone who lifts some files or does light paperwork in an office requiring some degree of carrying or lifting. It may also be a type of security guard who does light lifting as part of their duties on the job. There are a million examples of light work, but you should just be aware that the Social Security Administration will identify your past relevant work as light if it's between five and 15 pounds.

Medium work is usually defined as anything between 20 to 50 pounds. A waitress or a waiter may be considered someone who does medium work.

Heavy work can include labor jobs, mechanics, welders, or any other type of job that requires lifting between 50 and 100 pounds or more.

Very Heavy work includes jobs that require lifting over 100 pounds.

If a person can do very heavy work, then SSA will also determine that the person can do heavy, medium, light, and sedentary work.

Do you remember what we have discussed in the 5-Step Sequential Evaluation for determining if an individual is disabled? Well, exertional levels play a huge role when it comes to steps 4 and 5. Your exertional level to perform work, as well as your age, education, and whether or not your past relevant work provided you with transferable skills or not is considered. These are called "the grids" and are a part of step 4 and step 5 of the 5-step sequential evaluation used to determine if you should be found disabled or not.

Understanding the different exertional levels of the sedentary, light, medium, and heavy will help you understand how Social Security will categorize your past relevant work and whether or not Social Security will be able to find other work for you in the national economy.

What they do is they try to match up your exertional level from your past relevant work with another potential job at the same exertional level to see if you can perform that new job.

Your attorney will be familiar with exertional levels and how it plays into either approving or denying your case.

Tip #83: Handing Over the Baton

We all enjoy watching the Olympics or track and field events when they come to town.

One of the tracks and field events often require a team of four runners who carry a baton before the race can be completed.

Each runner takes one lap around the track, holding a baton, and then hands the baton to the next runner to complete the next lap around the track.

The same goes for the Social Security Administration. A baton is passed from SSA department to SSA department before a decision can be made.

The first runner on the track is the Social Security District Office. The District Office is the location that accepts the application, processes the application, comment, and make determinations on income, resources, credits, residency, and citizenship. Once these areas are determined, the Social Security Administration passes the baton to the Disability Determination Services.

The Disability Determination Services takes the baton and runs with it. Their task is to request all of the medical records necessary to decide if you are disabled or not. Not only will they request medical records, but they will also send you forms to complete, like the Function Report and the Work History report, as well as the schedule for a Consultative Examination with the Social Security doctors. Once all of that is completed, the baton is handed back to the Social Security District Office to send out an award letter if you've been approved or denied benefits.

If the case is approved, the baton is passed to the SSA Payment Center; the Payment Center will then process your payments out of Baltimore, Maryland, and make sure that you get your benefit payments, as well as the back-pay.

If the case is not approved, a request for Reconsideration must be filed within 60 days of the denial. And the baton is passed back to the Disability Determination Services to process the Disability Insurance period once again. The Disability Determination Services will request medical records, send you forms, and possibly even send you to a consultative examination.

Once the decision is made on the Disability Insurance, the baton is passed back to the Social Security Administration to send out the award letter if you've been approved or denied.

Finally, once approved, the baton is passed to the SSA Payment Center in order to process the payments. Suppose the case is not approved at the Reconsideration level and a request for a hearing before an Administrative Law Judge is filed. In that case, the baton is passed to the Office of Hearings and Operations, where the Judge resides.

The Office of Hearings and Operations is responsible for scheduling your hearing, commenting, and preparing the Electronic Records Express file for the Judge. That means that all of your medical records must be submitted to the Office of Hearings and Operations, and they will upload them to the electronic file for the Judge to view. Once again, if the case is approved, then the baton is passed to the Payment Center for processing of payments,

If the case is not approved, the Judge will send you the denied decision, and you have 60 days to request an appeal before the Appeals Council.

If the Appeals Council gets the baton, its role is to determine if there was an error of law made by the Judge's decision. They will not do any fact-finding. Instead, all they will be looking for is whether or not the Judge made an error of law. If an error of law is made, the Appeals Council will either approve the case or pass the baton back to the Administrative Law Judge in order to have a supplemental hearing or a completely new hearing to determine if you're disabled or not. If the Appeals Council is denied, your next option is the Federal District courts.

If your case makes it to the Federal District Court, you probably already have been involved in the process for two years and are likely losing patience. Don't give up, as the pot of money is growing every day. The federal district court will review all aspects of the case to determine whether the case should be approved or remanded back down for another hearing.

As you can see, the passing of the baton in chronological order of the processing of your claim is a very important part of understanding the Social Security disability process.

Tip #84: Resources

One of the main differences between Supplemental Security Income and Social Security Disability Insurance is the "Resources" eligibility criteria.

Resources are basically what you own and what has value. This can include cash, bank accounts, stocks, land, life insurance with a cash value, personal property, vehicles, or anything else you own, which can be changed into cash and used for food or shelter.

With SSDI, there are **no** limits on resources, and you can have a million dollars in the bank and as many properties and vehicles as you want.

However, with SSI, certain resource requirements must be met to be approved for the program.

In general, you cannot have more than $2,000 in the bank if you are single or more than $3,000 in the bank if you are married.

The following resources are also *not* counted by SSA:

- The home you live in and the land it is on;

- One vehicle, regardless of value, if you or a member of your household use it for transportation;

- Household goods and personal effects (e.g., your wedding and engagement rings);

- Life insurance policies with a combined face value of $1,500 or less;

- Burial spaces for you or your immediate family;

- Burial funds for you and your spouse, each valued at $1,500 or less;

- The property you or your spouse use in a trade or business or on your job if you work for someone else;

- If you are disabled or blind, money or property you have set aside under a plan to achieve self-support (pass); and

- Up to $100,000 of funds in an achieving a better life experience (able) account established through a state-able program.

Unless you meet the resources criteria, you will not be eligible for SSI.

Even if you are found medically disabled, you still have to remember that SSI is a needs-based program. As such, unless you meet the resource requirements, you cannot get approved.

Always ensure you are clear on your resource levels before applying for disability benefits or risk being denied.

Tip #85: Supplemental Security Income

Here we are again. Back to SSI Review. Why? Because I find that each time I review the topic, some of you pick up new information and details that you missed the first time around.

There are primarily two different programs that a disabled person can apply for with the Social Security Administration. The first is Supplemental Security Income (SSI), and the second is Social Security Disability Insurance (SSDI).

Supplemental Security Income (SSI) is a Federal income supplement program funded by general tax revenues (not Social Security taxes).

It is designed to help aged, blind, and disabled people who have little or no income, and it provides cash to meet basic needs for food, clothing, and shelter.

Anyone aged 18-65 or older, blind or disabled, is eligible for SSI. The Claimant must have limited income, is a resident of one of 50 states, commonly is not absent from the country for a full calendar month or 30 consecutive days or more, and is not confined to an institution such as a hospital or prison at the government's expense and meets other applications and meets other requirements such as income and resources.

In general, resources include cash, bank accounts, stocks, lands, vehicles, personal property, and life insurance. Part of the benefits of having SSI is that you get monthly payments from your state and Medicaid from the first month, but you are not eligible. It is important to note that anyone with an unsatisfied Felony or arrest warrant is unsuitable for SSI.

As mentioned earlier on in the introduction to this book, SSI does not let you go back a year from your application date. You can only move forward. SSI does not pay out "Auxiliary Benefits" to your children. SSI applications cannot be done online, only by paper or with a Social Security Employee over the telephone. And finally, in almost every state, Medicaid is awarded with SSI — not Medicare.

Below are some of the eligibility criteria:

Who Is Eligible For SSI?

- Anyone who is: aged (age 65 or older), blind, or disabled

- And, who: has limited income; has limited resources; is a US citizen or national, or in one of the certain categories of aliens

- Additionally, the SSI beneficiary must be a resident of one of the 50 States, the District of Columbia, or the Northern Mariana Islands

- Cannot be absent from the country for a full calendar month or for 30 consecutive days or more

- Cannot be confined to an institution (such as a hospital or prison) at the government's expense

- Gives SSA permission to contact any financial institution and request any financial records about you

- Files an application

- Meets certain other requirements.

What Is "Blindness" For An Adult Or Child?

'BLINDNESS' MEANS THAT you have a central visual acuity for a distance of 20/200 or less in your better eye with the use of a correcting lens, or you have a visual field limitation in your better eye, such that the widest diameter of the visual field subtends an angle no greater than 20 degrees.

What Are The Resource Limits?

- A single individual cannot have more than $2,000 in the bank;

- A married couple cannot have more than $3,000 in the bank.

IT SHOULD BE NOTED that if you give away a resource or sell it for less than it is worth in order to reduce your resources below the SSI resource limit, you may be ineligible for SSI for up to 36 months.

In short, SSI is really a backup option for those of you who do not have the requisite 40 work credits that are needed for SSDI. It is a program that is needs-based and which will provide you with a flat benefits amount which is the same as what all other SSI recipients get in your state.

Tip #86: Social Security Disability Insurance

Social Security Disability Insurance pays benefits to you and to certain members of your family if you are insured, meaning that you've worked long enough and paid Social Security taxes.

In general, this means that you have 40 active work credits, which you've acquired throughout your career. In addition, you are eligible for Medicare 24 months after your entitlement date, not including the five months for the eligibility.

In addition, your children, if 18 years or younger and still in school, are eligible for Auxiliary Benefits, which is a portion of your monthly benefits. Your benefits will not be reduced at all, but your children who are 18 and under and still in school will receive a portion of those benefits.

With an SSDI application, unlike with SSI, you can go retroactive 12 months from the application period, which means that if you believe that you became disabled in June 2021, even if you were filing your application in June 2022, you can go retroactive 12 months toward your Onset date back in 2021 and collect up to 12 months of backpay benefits.

This is not the case with the SSI. SSI only allows you to move forward from the application date, but as we just mentioned, SSDI allows you to move backward 12 months or more.

If you have the choice between SSI and SSDI, it is much better to apply for SSDI as the benefits package is more extensive.

It should be known that there are no income or resource levels for SSDI.

You can have a million dollars in the bank and still be eligible for SSDI.

People always ask me if they can get married while they're on SSDI, and the answer is yes. Because there is no income or resource eligibility criteria, everything is based on your own earning record.

Tip# 87: Consultative Examinations

At some point during your application or appeals process, your Social Security DDS worker may send you for a Consultative Examination (CE).

In general, Consultative Examination can either be a psychological examination, a physical examination, or both.

In this chapter, we will be discussing what you can expect at a physical examination by the Social Security Administration.

You have to remember that these examinations are completed by the lowest bidding contractor. In other words, it means that SSA contracts out the Consultative Examinations to medical provider "bidders," who are usually selected based on the price they will charge per each examination. The lowest bidder usually gets the contract. So, truth be told, don't expect too much from the examiner, or the examination.

You are not going to have a full comprehensive examination, you are not going to have blood work, and you're not going to have any extensive imaging necessarily done, except for maybe x-rays, if at all.

The examination will last no more than 20-30 minutes. They are watching everything. They are watching to see if you were able to drive to the examination, or if you had to take a ride from a family member or take a car service. They are watching your appearance to see if you are clean, hygienic, and properly dressed or if you have difficulty with your basic hygiene. They will take your weight, they will take your height, they will take your blood pressure, but that's about it. They will not perform any laboratory tests or provide or ask you to provide a urine sample. They may ask you to change and to jump on the table, and they are watching to see if, in fact, you are able to get on the table and off the table without assistance.

They're looking to see if you walked in with a cane, a crutch, a walker, or a wheelchair. You have to let them know if you use any assisted devices during the day, whether that be an oxygen tank, a brace, a C-PAP machine, a sole insert for your shoes, or anything else. They will ask you to walk toe to heel, and they will check your range of motion and your shoulders, and your legs. This is a very important examination, and it is important that you let Social Security doctors know exactly what is wrong with you.

You should provide them with a proper diagnosis and/or a list all your impairments. Don't just say that you are in pain or that your body hurts. You have to provide a diagnosis for what is wrong with you.

You should provide them with the names of any hospitals that you've been admitted to in the last two years, so that they can request the records.

You should write down the names of the medications on a piece of paper and provide that to the examiner. As well as any side effects that the medications cause you.

And most importantly, you must write down **all of the symptoms** that you're having, no matter what they are or how severe they are, to make sure that they're in the report.

Remember, not only is SSA looking at your medical records when they review your application, but they are looking at the report that is generated by the Consultative Examiner.

The mental examinations are also very short, and those can generally either be performed in-person or over a video-conference call. The examiner will ask you questions about your mental history, as well as your family's mental history. They will test your memory and concentration, by asking you certain questions like "who is the President of the United State?" Or, they may say the color "blue" and ask you to remember that word, and then circle back to that word after a few minutes. They may ask you count up or down in a particular format. They are not trying to test you like you are in school. They are simply trying to gauge your memory, concentration and skills.

They will want information of how you interact with the general public, co-workers or supervisors. They will want to know if you can handle changes in the workplaces. They will want to know if you can handle your own finances, and other facts relating to your mental health.

I can tell you from doing thousands of hearings that these Consultative Examination reports <u>are</u> reviewed by the Judges, and that they <u>do</u> play an important role at the hearing.

Make sure that you attend your Consultative Examination at all costs. This is a very important piece of the Social Security disability process. You don't want to give any reason at all for SSA to deny you because you failed to attend your Consultative Examination. That would be a big no-no.

Tip# 88: Depression and Bipolar

Each year, more than 3 million Americans experience Bipolar Disorder.

Bipolar Disorder is commonly classified as Bipolar 1 and Bipolar 2.

They are very different.

Bipolar Disorder is a mental health disorder that causes people to have extreme mood swings. People with bipolar disorder experience periods of emotional highs and emotional lows. Periods of emotional highs are known as mania; its symptoms are feeling overconfident, out of the world, extreme happiness, and becoming too talkative. In comparison, the depressive period's symptoms are hopelessness, guilt, low energy, sadness, and suicide, suicidal thoughts.

The episodes of Bipolar 1 are often more severe than those of Bipolar 2. People with the latter may engage in behavior extremely harmful to their well-being, such as spending lots of money on things they don't need or having unsafe sex with multiple partners. Bipolar 2 is often less severe and noticeable. They may experience depressive episodes, but they won't need hospitalization. Yet, their symptoms may disrupt their daily activities. In comparison, people with Bipolar 1 may experience major depressive episodes that increase the risk of hospitalization and suicide.

I recently represented a Claimant before a Judge who had Bipolar Disorder. She described her mania as cycling between super high and super low, depending on the day of the week. Some days, she felt high as a kite and able to accomplish anything. However, there were other days when she felt so low that she couldn't even come out of bed which is typical for a person with a bipolar diagnosis. These moods swings could last days, weeks or months at a time. She also experienced crying spells, mood swings, hopelessness, weight loss and guilt. She could not interact with the public, co-workers or even supervisors and had poor memory and concentration.

Luckily, we won this case before the Judge because of the Social Security Listing 12.04.

The Social Security Adult Listing 12.04 states the following:

12.04 Depressive, bipolar, and related disorders (see 12.00B3), satisfied by A and B, or A and C:

A. Medical documentation of the requirements of paragraph 1 or 2:

1. Depressive disorder is characterized by five or more of the following

a. Depressed mood;

b. Diminished interest in almost all activities;

c. Appetite disturbance with change in weight;

d. Sleep disturbance;

e. Observable psychomotor agitation or retardation;

f. Decreased energy;

g. Feelings of guilt or worthlessness;

h. Difficulty concentrating or thinking; or

i. Thoughts of death or suicide.

2. Bipolar disorder is characterized by three or more of the following:

a. Pressured speech;

b. Flight of ideas;

c. Inflated self-esteem;

d. Decreased need for sleep;

e. Distractibility;

f. Involvement in activities that have a high probability of painful consequences that are not recognized; or

g. Increase in goal-directed activity or psychomotor agitation.

AND

B. Extreme limitation of one, or marked limitation of two, of the following areas of mental functioning (see 12.00F[8]):

1. Understand, remember, or apply information (see 12.00E1[9]).

2. Interact with others (see 12.00E2[10]).

3. Concentrate, persist, or maintain pace (see 12.00E3[11]).

4. Adapt or manage oneself (see 12.00E4[12]).

OR

C. Your mental disorder in this listing category is "serious and persistent;" that is, you have a medically documented history of the existence of the disorder over a period of at least 2 years, and there is evidence of both:

---

8. https://www.ssa.gov/disability/professionals/bluebook/
12.00-MentalDisorders-Adult.htm#a5c02393e59c943d6a75a9241140faca312_00F

9. https://www.ssa.gov/disability/professionals/bluebook/
12.00-MentalDisorders-Adult.htm#a5c02393e59c943d6a75a9241140faca312_00E1

10. https://www.ssa.gov/disability/professionals/bluebook/
12.00-MentalDisorders-Adult.htm#a5c02393e59c943d6a75a9241140faca312_00E2

11. https://www.ssa.gov/disability/professionals/bluebook/
12.00-MentalDisorders-Adult.htm#a5c02393e59c943d6a75a9241140faca312_00E3

12. https://www.ssa.gov/disability/professionals/bluebook/
12.00-MentalDisorders-Adult.htm#a5c02393e59c943d6a75a9241140faca312_00E4

1. Medical treatment, mental health therapy, psychosocial support(s), or a highly structured setting(s) that is ongoing and that diminishes the symptoms and signs of your mental disorder (see 12.00G2b[13]); and

2. Marginal adjustment, that is, you have minimal capacity to adapt to changes in your environment or to demands that are not already part of your daily life (see 12.00G2c[14]).

The best way to win a bipolar case is to see a therapist for 12 months in a row and make sure that those medical records are released to the Social Security Administration.

You must be under prescribed medication regimens.

There can be no drugs or alcohol on your record.

You need to get a non-exertional residual functional capacity questionnaire completed by your doctor or therapist outlining your restrictions and limitations. I have included a sample in the Appendix of this book.

And most importantly, you need to have a great attorney who can present your case to the Judge.

Bipolar Disorder is a very serious medical condition, but luckily Social Security disability benefits can provide some relief for those people who suffer from the Disorder.

---

13. https://www.ssa.gov/disability/professionals/bluebook/

 12.00-MentalDisorders-Adult.htm#a5c02393e59c943d6a75a9241140faca312_00G2b

14. https://www.ssa.gov/disability/professionals/bluebook/

 12.00-MentalDisorders-Adult.htm#a5c02393e59c943d6a75a9241140faca312_00G2c

TIP #89: Never Expose Yourself to the Judge

Here's a true story that actually occurred with one of my clients. I was at a hearing, and the client was a young lady suffering from less severe psychological and emotional problems. She regularly cried and was depressed and unstable.

At one point, the Judge asked her why she was so depressed. She immediately began to unstrap her bra straps and pulled up her shirt, and exposed her breasts to the Judge in front of the whole courtroom.

She stated, *"If you had small breasts like me, wouldn't you also be depressed every single day. I want to have big breasts."*

The Judge had her handcuffed, and she was escorted out of the room. Needless to say, she did not win her case.

This is a true story, which I personally witnessed in the courtroom. **The moral of the story is "Never expose yourself to the Judge."**

Tip #90: Appropriate Clothing

As previously discussed in this book, you must show respect to the Judge when in court.

You must dress respectfully for the courts. You don't necessarily need to come in a suit and tie, but you certainly need to be dressed respectably.

One time, after the Los Angeles riots in 1992, I was representing a Claimant who was very anti-police and pro-civil rights for African American community. He was wearing a shirt that said in capital letters, *"Fuck the Police."* When he showed up in court, I asked him, "What are you wearing?"

He answered, "I'm wearing my favorite T-shirt."

I said, "Are you insane? You cannot wear that shirt in front of a Judge that says, *"Fuck The Police."* You need to go to the bathroom, and you need to turn it inside out."

He said, "Why?"

I answered, "Because you're not showing proper respect to the court and to the Judge."

He was very upset at the instructions I gave. But he went ahead and slipped his shirt around so that the offensive message was not visible to the Judge or to the courts. Another time, I had a gentleman who showed up with so many gold necklaces and so many diamonds. You would think he needed a security guard just to walk down the street. I asked, "How did you go ahead and afford all jewelry?"

And he replied, "I sell drugs on the side."

I made him take off all the jewelry before he appeared before the court.

The moral of the story is to always wear appropriate clothes to the hearing and look respectable to the Judge.

Tip #91: The Invisible Illness

What do mental health conditions, rheumatoid arthritis, lupus, fibromyalgia, diabetes all have in common?

The answer is they're called the "invisible illness."

It means that from the outside, it is very difficult, if not impossible, to identify or determine that the person is suffering from an illness. However, inside, they are suffering terribly. There are too many "invisible illnesses" to list.

Whether it is crying spells, staying in bed until late afternoon, or being unable to perform activities of daily activities like shopping, dressing, bathing, cooking, and using a vehicle, invisible illnesses affect millions of Americans each year.

The only way to win a case when you have an invisible illness is to have medical records, medical records, and medical records.

You must have documented all the symptoms of your invisible illness in your medical records. It means that every time you go to the doctor and you must discuss your case with the professional, you must make sure that the therapist is writing down all of your invisible illness symptoms. The invisible illness becomes visible to the Judge through the medical records.

A person does not need to lose a case based on an invisible illness. They just need to have medical records that back up and support the "invisible illness" if they want to win their case.

Tip #92: Direct Deposits

There are two ways that you can get paid once your case is approved.

You can receive a monthly Direct Express payment from Social Security, or you can receive a direct deposit into your bank account. Because most people have bank accounts these days, the preferred method of payment is through direct deposit.

As mentioned above, this can be arranged directly through the Social Security Administration.

All that you need to do is provide Social Security Administration with your routing number and bank account number, and they will automatically begin depositing the monthly benefit amount into your checking account.

I highly recommend that everyone sets up with their local SSA District Office to receive their payments by direct deposit.

It should also be noted that SSA pays benefits monthly. The benefits are paid in the month that follows the month for which they are due. For example, you would receive your July benefit in August.

Additionally, the day of the month you receive your benefit payment depends on the birth date of the person for whose earning record you receive benefits. Individuals born between the 1st and 10th of the month are paid on the Second Wednesday, if born between the 11th-20th of the month are paid on the Third Wednesday and on the Fourth Wednesday if born between the 21st and the 31st of the month.

Tip #93: Electronic Records Express (ERE)

According to www.ssa.gov[15], Electronic Records Express or the "ERE" *"is an initiative by Social Security and state Disability Determination Services (DDS) to offer electronic options for submitting health and school records related to disability claims."*

At this time, you can choose the method of sending the information that works best for you:

- Online to Social Security's secure website; or

- By fax to your state DDS or to Social Security.

The records you send are automatically associated with the applicant's unique disability claim folder."

I have to say that the implementation of the ERE was a huge step forward for SSA. In the "old days," all medical records had to be faxed or sent by hard-copy delivery to the OHO offices. Now, the ERE will allow you to:

- Send patient, client, and student records at your convenience;

- Submit information directly to your state DDS or Social Security, helping to expedite the decision on your patient's or student's disability claim;

- Save copying and postage costs;

- Eliminate the need for follow-up due to mail transit time; and

- Start the reimbursement process sooner.

Anyone who provides health or school records to Social Security or the DDS can use the ERE such as:

- Medical providers (including hospitals, clinics, doctors, and health information managers);

- School professionals; and

- Third parties, such as attorneys and claimant representatives.

---

15. http://www.ssa.gov

All Electronic Records Express options are free of charge. In fact, you may save time and money by transmitting your records electronically.

It should be noted that the website has restricted access. *Only authorized users can access the secure website by using their assigned user ID and password.* Also, data transmission is protected by employing 128-bit or higher secure socket layer (SSL) encryption, which is the industry encryption standard for providing network security.

In order to use the ERE, just call the Social Security Electronic Records Express Help Desk at 1-866-691-3061. This number will be staffed from 7am – 7pm EST, Monday thru Friday. After-hours, questions about new ERE account registration may be emailed to electronic-records-express@ssa.gov.

Tip# 94: Elevating Your Legs

Eventually, there is going to come a time during the disability hearing when the Judge turns to the Vocational Experts to get two pieces of important information.

The first piece of information is whether you can return to your old job, and the second piece of important information is whether a hypothetical individual with the same age, education, work history and residual functional capacity as you can get any other job in the national economy.

In almost all cases, the Vocational Expert will be able to list 3 potential jobs that are available in the national economy. It is very important that you make sure that your attorney gets the Vocational Expert down to zero jobs. I cannot emphasize this enough! There are many legal techniques on how to do that. In this chapter, we are going to focus on one technique which is the need to elevate your feet.

The best way to do that is to focus on residual functional capacity. How long can you stand? How far can you walk? How long can you sit, and how much can you carry?

The question of how long you can sit is a very important question because if the Judge expects you to work eight hours a day or 40 hours a week. You're going to need to show that you can only sit or stand or walk for a limited amount of time. Now, there is a trick that is used by myself and other competent and experienced disability attorneys that deals with accommodations at the workplace. Meaning if you can show that your medical needs are so severe that it would require an accommodation that the employer cannot accommodate, then the Judge will have to find that there are zero jobs available in the hypothetical that is posed to the Vocational Expert.

Specifically, even though you might be able to sit for prolonged periods of time if your legs are elevated, that is a specific accommodation that must be met by your employers in order to keep you employed. The trick is that you need to show the Vocational Expert and the Judge that you need to raise your legs 24 to 36 inches or higher off of the ground for at least 4-6 hours a day.

That doesn't mean that you can just give that testimony and automatically will it to be true. Your medical records must notate that you have a medical need to elevate your legs that height for a specific amount of time each day... or suffer the medical consequences.

Once you establish that your legs are under medical supervision, you need to be 24 to 36 inches off the ground or waist level. The Vocational Expert will find that there are no other jobs that can be performed in the hypothetical that is presented by the Judge.

Why? Because this is an accommodation that cannot be made, and such a person will be found under SSA vocational rules to be unemployable.

Think about it.

Most office desks have a cubicle or have a limited amount of space. They are not designed for a worker to elevate their legs 24 to 36 inches. If you're ever interested in getting your Vocational Expert easily down to zero jobs, you must show that when seated, your legs have to be elevated 24 to 36 inches, for at least 4 hours a day.

Of course, this tactic does not work with psychological or mental health issues. There are other legal questions for those hypotheticals. This is just one example.

But, if you fall into that category of impairments that require elevating your legs 24 to 36 inches off the ground, and you present that hypothetical to the Vocational Expert, you stand a good chance of getting the Vocational Expert down to zero jobs.

Tip#95: Continuing Disability Reviews (CDR)

For some reason, I have a feeling that many of you are going to read this chapter several times.

Why?

Because getting approved for disability benefits is only the beginning. Once you have been approved, at one point or another, SSA is going to send you a letter saying that it is time for your Continuing Disability Review (CDR). Perhaps you have already received this CDR notice from SSA.

In short, what SSA is trying to determine when they do a CDR is if you still continue to have a disabling condition or if you can return back to work. You may have had surgery, gone to therapy, started working again, or recovered. Hopefully, you are feeling better.

If SSA determines that you are no longer disabled or blind and/or you are working above Substantial Gainful Activity, your benefits will stop.

The law requires SSA to perform a medical CDR at least once every three years. If, however, you have a medical condition that is not expected to improve, SSA will still review your case once every five to seven years. In almost all cases, SSA will contact you to obtain updated information about your condition using the SSA-454 (Continuing Disability Review Report) or SSA-455 (Disability Update Report) form.

The trick to CDRs is to be prepared for them.

It is not a secret.

Eventually, you will get notified that it is your turn for a CDR.

All you need to do to easily pass your CDR, and continue to receive your disability benefits, is to continue going to the doctor during the entire period that you are disabled and receiving benefits — which you are probably doing anyways. That really is all you need to know.

Unfortunately, most attorneys do not assist with CDR, since there is really no way for them to get paid on this service.

No different than when you applied, SSA is going to request your records and review them. In most cases, as long as you have been going to the doctor, you stand a good chance of being re-approved.

Make sure that all updated providers, medications and other pertinent information is provided during this review.

Tip #96: Off-Task Time

In the final part of your disability hearing, the Judge will turn to the Vocational Expert who will be asked a certain amount of questions to determine if a hypothetical scenario of someone like you with the same residual functional capacity, can get any of the jobs in the national economy.

What many people don't realize is that there is another strategy, tip, and tactic to get the Vocational Expert down to zero jobs.

The standard workplace provides a 15-minute break in the morning and a 15-minute break in the afternoon. The tactic employed requires you to ask the Vocational Expert what would happen if the hypothetical person needed more than a 15-minute break in the morning and more than a 15-minute break in the afternoon. Or, if they were required to take an unscheduled break away from their work station during the work day. This is called "Off-Task" time.

The vocational rules state that if a hypothetical person with the same residual functional capacity as you is going to be off-task more than 10% of the time during a workday, then they are considered vocationally unemployable. This will always get the Vocational Expert down to zero jobs.

It isn't enough to just show that the hypothetical person will be off task 10% or more of the time; you need to explain to the Judge *why* the hypothetical person would be off task more than 10% of the time.

Are you tired?

Do you need to elevate your feet?

Do you need to take frequent breaks to go to the bathroom?

Are you not able to work around public coworkers or supervisors?

Do you get anxiety attacks?

Do you need to use a nebulizer?

What about checking your blood sugar levels and taking injections?

There are a host of other medical problems which could result in you requiring more than a 15-minute break in the morning and a 15-minute break in the afternoon.

All you need to show is that the hypothetical person with the same residual functional capacity as you would be off-task more than 10% of the time, and you will get the Vocational Expert down to zero jobs every single time.

Tip #97: Absenteeism

As we've discussed multiple times in this book, the Judge is going to go to the Vocational Expert at the end of the hearing to determine 2 items:

1. If a hypothetical individual who has the same age, education, height, weight and same residual functional capacity as you can return to your old job, and
2. If a hypothetical individual who has the same age, education, height, weight and same residual functional capacity as you can get any other job in the national economy.

If the Vocational Expert can establish that a hypothetical individual who has the same age, education, height, weight and same residual functional capacity as is able to find other employment, then you will lose your case because there are other jobs that this hypothetical person can potentially perform.

There is, however, a tactic that can be used to always get the Vocational Expert down to zero jobs.

That tactic includes showing the amount of absenteeism or attendance this hypothetical person would have at an employed job. Whether or not this hypothetical individual would be absent because of doctor's appointment, to a medical procedure, or are just not feeling well enough to work a certain amount of times a month, that will be enough to get the Vocational Expert down to zero jobs.

What is the magic number?

The magic number is more than two times a month.

If you can show that that this hypothetical individual will be absent more than two times a month, the Vocational Expert will have to show under the vocational rules that this individual is unemployable, and you will always get the Vocational Expert down to zero jobs.

This is a tremendous strategic move that works every time to get the Vocational Expert down to zero jobs.

All you have to show is that this hypothetical person will be absent more than two times a month because of medical conditions, or doctor appointment, and you will be good to go.

Tip #98: "As if" it's a bad day.

At some point during the application or appeals process, your Disability Determination Services worker will probably send you an Adult Function Report to complete as part of the application or appeal process.

The function report is an eight-page document that basically records your Activities of Daily Living or ADLs.

The questions are not difficult and are very straightforward. They basically ask how you spend your day from the time you get up in the morning until the time you go to sleep at night.

This form is usually filled out by the Claimant and not the attorney because the attorney is not always sure about what exactly you do during the day or your restrictions and limitations during the course of the day.

I always give the following advice when it comes to completing the function. The advice is as follows:

You have to tell the truth, the whole truth, and nothing but the truth, but I want you to give answers "as if" you're having a bad day.

Why do I say having a bad day? We all have "good days" and "bad days." If you had to go to work and you were having a "bad day" in terms of how you felt medically, you would call in sick. That is the answer you need to give on the function report.

SSA needs to know the extent of your restrictions and limitations, and that can only be articulated if you report how you feel on a bad day.

You don't want to fill out the function report as if you're having a good day. You want to fill out the function report as if you're having a bad day.

I know that it is difficult for many people to step out of their armor and discuss their restrictions and limitations with strangers.

I cannot emphasize enough how important it is for you to fill out the function report "as if" you're having a bad day.

This includes, but is not limited to, whether you can dress on your own, whether you can bathe and shower and take care of basic hygiene on your own, whether you can cook and clean and do other chores around the house, whether you need help getting out of bed, whether you need help with money or driving or any other activity of daily living.

You must get all that information down on the function report so your analyst can review it during the time of the application and appeal, and the Judge can reference him back at the time of the hearing.

Tip #99: 15 Years of Employment History

During the course of your application or appeal, your Social Security Disability Determination Services worker is not only going send you an Adult Function Report, but they will also send you a Work History report.

The Work History report is a very important document.

It is important because it outlines for SSA the different types of jobs you have had, the type of work you did, the length of time you did it, and the exertional requirements needed to complete these tasks at your job.

The key is that it only goes back 15 years.

Social Security will not look beyond 15 years of your work history.

As such, it is important that you outline the 15 years of work history that you have for Social Security to review. Once again, these are straightforward and simple questions, and you have to do your best.

Try to answer these questions as simply as possible.

The work history report will generally ask the name of the company that you worked at, the title that you had at the job, your salary, and the residual functional capacity skills you needed in order to perform this job, meaning how much you had to stand, how much you had to sit, how much you had to lift or carry, how far you had to walk, whether you needed to bend, kneel, stoop, or crawl or push or pull.

Only 15 years of work history matters to Social Security, and that is what you should report to the best of your ability.

This is not an optional form.

SSA will deny you if they do not receive this form completed.

Tip #100: Psychological Consultative Examinations

During the course of your application or appeal, your Social Security Administration Disability Determination Services worker will not only send you a Function Report and a Work History Report, but they may also send you for a "Consultative Examination" with the Social Security doctors.

There are generally two types of Consultative Examinations; a Psychological examination and a physical examination. In this chapter, we will be discussing the mental examination.

What can you expect at your Psychological Consultative Examination?

You can expect the examination to last 20 to 30 minutes, and they will ask you a host of questions to gauge your mental competency.

They will be watching what you wear and if you are appropriately dressed or whether you are disheveled.

They will look at your hygiene to see if you are bathing and showering or if you are unkempt; they will look to see if you drove or were able to drive to the examination or if you needed to get a lift from a friend, a family, or a car service.

They will ask you some questions to test your memory and concentration.

They may ask you to remember the word apple or the color blue, and then five minutes later, they will ask you if you can recall the same things. They may ask you, who is the president of the United States? They may ask you what country we are living in. They may ask you to do basic calculations again to determine your memory and concentration. They may ask you to count up by 5s. 5, 10, 15, 20, 25, or they may ask you to count down by tens, 50, 40, 30, 20, 10.

They will ask you about drugs and alcohol and if you are using any or when the last time you used it was.

And they will ask you about any medications you're taking and their side effects.

It is very important for you to tell the examiner the diagnosis you have if you know them. Meaning if you know that you have a major depressive disorder or generalized anxiety disorder, or schizophrenia, you need to provide the proper diagnosis.

You also need to go ahead and provide any names of hospitals to which you've been admitted for psychiatric evaluation in the last two years.

Again, you need to provide the medication list that you are currently taking.

And most importantly, you need to get down all of your symptoms during the psychiatric examination that you have. If you cry during the day and have crying spells, you need to let them know that you are crying. If you have feelings of guilt or worthlessness, you need to let them know that you have feelings of guilt and worthless. Has there been a change, an increase, or a decrease in your weight?

Do you have suicidal thoughts? Do you have thoughts of hurting other people? How is your interaction with the public, with supervisors, or with coworkers? How is your memory and concentration? These are all questions that must be answered during the psychological and mental examination. Additional questions may include, do you hear voices?

How often do you hear the voices? What are those voices telling you? Do you have anxiety attacks? How often do you have anxiety attacks? Describe an anxiety attack, et cetera. Any psychological or mental problems that you have must be provided and described in detail to the examiner.

In many cases, the Examiner will also decide if you need a "Representative Payee" or not to help you handle your benefits, if you are approved. There are many people who, for various reasons, require assistance when handling money. The Examiner will make this recommendation at the time of your examination.

This is your one shot to let Social Security know exactly how you're feeling in your own words.

It is a very important appointment that you really need to keep.

SSA and the Judge at your hearing will look at this report and will determine how much weight should be given to the examination findings and then weigh those findings in the report against other medical evidence in the record.

Tip #101: You made it!

Congratulations! You made it to the 101st tip to winning your Social Security disability benefits.

It is only because of your determination that you made it this far. Your determination to go to the doctor, your determination to undergo medical treatment, your determination to receive laboratory tests, as well as other medical procedures.

If you have made it this far, you are one of the few people who have the determination necessary to win your Social Security disability case.

I hope you've enjoyed these 101 tips, and I assure you that by following these 101 tips, you will have a substantially greater chance of winning your Social Security disability case.

My final tip to everyone, if it isn't already obvious to you, is that you should hire an attorney to help you with your Social Security disability case.

Once again, no fee has to be paid to the attorney if the attorney cannot win your case. Only if the attorney wins your case, then you have to pay the fees of the legal services, which is either 25% of the first check or $7,200. I wish you the best of luck on your journey to secure your Social Security disability benefits.

Just like Rocky Balboa raised his arms in victory after running up the stairs in Rocky...

...I want you all to raise your hands in victory when you win your claim for disability benefits.

Finale

Congratulations! You did it!

You now have 101 tips to win your Social Security disability claim for benefits.

We've discussed everything that you need to know about how to win your case.

We've reviewed the screening process, and we reviewed the application process.

We've reviewed the Disability Determinations Service and its role in the overall process.

We've reviewed the appeals process, and we've reviewed the hearing process.

We've even discussed the SSA Appeals Counsel and the Federal District Court.

We've covered the function reports, the work history reports, and consultative examinations.

We've covered the importance of medical records, medical records, and medical records! And the importance of a residual functional capacity questionnaire by your doctor.

Most importantly, we've spent a substantial amount of time talking about the importance of having an experienced and qualified Social Security attorney assist you with your claim.

Again, my parting thought on the best way to win your Social Security disability claim is to hire and retain an experienced and qualified Social Security attorney. After all, this is a legal process in its nature, and you have tens of thousands of dollars at stake.

Find an attorney who has good reviews online and who has done several hundred cases before a disability Judge. The experience that they have in all steps of the application and appeals, and hearing process is unmatched.

If I can help, please reach out to me at:

www.AndBenefitsForAll.com[16]

And finally, above all else, please take care of yourselves and feel good!

I send my sincerest prayers and blessings to you for your good health.

---

16. http://www.AndBenefitsForAll.com

Appendix A: Listing of Impairments — Adult Listings (Part A)

The Listing of Impairments — Adult Listings contains medical criteria that apply to the evaluation of impairments in adults aged 18 and over.

While it was my original intention to include **<u>ALL</u>** of the Adult Listings in this book, the reality is that it added another 350+ pages to the book, and I felt that it would be too overwhelming and confusing for the reader.

As such, my best advice is to go online and google "SSA ADULT LISTINGS."

The complete list of all medical listings will pop up in your search results, and you should simply click your medical condition to see if your medical impairments match up with the Social Security medical listing requirements.

Alternatively, speak to an attorney who can assist you in explaining the Adult Listing and how they may apply to your case.

Below is an Overview of the Adult Listings:

1.00[17]
Musculoskeletal Disorders[18]

2.00[19]
Special Senses and Speech[20]

3.00[21]
Respiratory Disorders[22]

4.00[23]
Cardiovascular System[24]

5.00[25]
Digestive System[26]

6.00[27]
Genitourinary Disorders[28]

7.00[29]
Hematological Disorders[30]

8.00[31]
Skin Disorders[32]

9.00[33]
Endocrine Disorders[34]

10.00[35]
Congenital Disorders that Affect Multiple Body Systems[36]

11.00[37]
Neurological Disorders[38]

12.00[39]
Mental Disorders[40]

13.00[41]
Cancer (Malignant Neoplastic Diseases)[42]

14.00[43]
Immune System Disorders[44]

---

17. https://www.ssa.gov/disability/professionals/bluebook/1.00-Musculoskeletal-Adult.htm

18. https://www.ssa.gov/disability/professionals/bluebook/1.00-Musculoskeletal-Adult.htm

19. https://www.ssa.gov/disability/professionals/bluebook/2.00-SpecialSensesandSpeech-Adult.htm

20. https://www.ssa.gov/disability/professionals/bluebook/2.00-SpecialSensesandSpeech-Adult.htm

21. https://www.ssa.gov/disability/professionals/bluebook/3.00-Respiratory-Adult.htm

22. https://www.ssa.gov/disability/professionals/bluebook/3.00-Respiratory-Adult.htm

23. https://www.ssa.gov/disability/professionals/bluebook/4.00-Cardiovascular-Adult.htm

24. https://www.ssa.gov/disability/professionals/bluebook/4.00-Cardiovascular-Adult.htm

25. https://www.ssa.gov/disability/professionals/bluebook/5.00-Digestive-Adult.htm

26. https://www.ssa.gov/disability/professionals/bluebook/5.00-Digestive-Adult.htm

27. https://www.ssa.gov/disability/professionals/bluebook/6.00-Genitourinary-Adult.htm

28. https://www.ssa.gov/disability/professionals/bluebook/6.00-Genitourinary-Adult.htm

29. https://www.ssa.gov/disability/professionals/bluebook/7.00-HematologicalDisorders-Adult.htm

30. https://www.ssa.gov/disability/professionals/bluebook/7.00-HematologicalDisorders-Adult.htm

31. https://www.ssa.gov/disability/professionals/bluebook/8.00-Skin-Adult.htm

32. https://www.ssa.gov/disability/professionals/bluebook/8.00-Skin-Adult.htm

33. https://www.ssa.gov/disability/professionals/bluebook/9.00-Endocrine-Adult.htm

34. https://www.ssa.gov/disability/professionals/bluebook/9.00-Endocrine-Adult.htm

35. https://www.ssa.gov/disability/professionals/bluebook/10.00-MultipleBody-Adult.htm

36. https://www.ssa.gov/disability/professionals/bluebook/10.00-MultipleBody-Adult.htm

37. https://www.ssa.gov/disability/professionals/bluebook/11.00-Neurological-Adult.htm

38. https://www.ssa.gov/disability/professionals/bluebook/11.00-Neurological-Adult.htm

39. https://www.ssa.gov/disability/professionals/bluebook/12.00-MentalDisorders-Adult.htm

40. https://www.ssa.gov/disability/professionals/bluebook/12.00-MentalDisorders-Adult.htm

41. https://www.ssa.gov/disability/professionals/bluebook/13.00-NeoplasticDiseases-Malignant-Adult.htm

42. https://www.ssa.gov/disability/professionals/bluebook/13.00-NeoplasticDiseases-Malignant-Adult.htm

43. https://www.ssa.gov/disability/professionals/bluebook/14.00-Immune-Adult.htm

44. https://www.ssa.gov/disability/professionals/bluebook/14.00-Immune-Adult.htm

Appendix B: Grid Rules

NOW THAT YOU HAVE REVIEWED your medical condition and determined that your impairment may not meet or equal a listing (See Appendix A), what do you do?

Well, all hope is not lost; the Grid rules are applied to give you yet another chance to provide your disability. This is called steps #4 and #5 of the 5-step Sequential Evaluation for determining disability.

The grid rules will navigate you and assist you in determining if an individual has a severe medically determinable physical or mental impairment and if the impairment prevents an individual from performing any of their past relevant work.

The Grids are set up as a series of charts, or Grids, if you will.

Before applying for the Grids, Social Security will decide what level of exertion you can perform in a specific work environment. This determination is generally made by the medical examiner or the Judge at the time of your hearing.

The categories are broken down from least level of exertion to most are sedentary, light, medium, heavy, and very heavy. In general, individuals who can perform at heavy or very heavy levels and don't have severe non-exertional limitations are generally not found disabled and therefore do not have a chart.

As such, the Grids only have charts for sedentary, light, and medium exertional levels.

Still with me?

I know this part can be confusing, which is why I recommend that you hire a qualified attorney to assist you with this legal grid analysis.

After Social Security makes a finding on your exertional level, they will use the corresponding chart and match your age, education, and your past work, which will either direct a finding of "disabled" or "not disabled."

What if you have both physical and mental impairments?

Well, if you have exertional (strength) and non-exertional limitations, the Social Security Administration will first determine if you can be found disabled based on the exertional limitations by themselves.

If the Grids, however, direct a finding of "not disabled," then Social Security will then consider any non-exertional limitations and how much those additional limitations would erode your ability to perform any jobs at that exertional level. The importance of age, education, and past work in your disability claim also plays into the Grid rules.

Your disability and how it limits you is not the only factor that decides whether you will be approved or not.

Exertional Levels

THE FIRST TASK IN UNDERSTANDING and using the Grids is to determine your Exertional level.

You need to make sure that you are looking at the correct Exertional level grid.

Simply find the Exertional level that you believe you are currently limited to based on the amount of weight you can lift, as well as how long you can stand or walk (they are labeled accordingly).

Make sure you are looking at the correct Grid based on your Exertional level. The Grids are provided immediately after this introduction to the Grids.

So, how do you determine your Exertional level, you ask?

In most cases, your treating doctors give an opinion on your Residual Function Capacity. I recommend using Residual Capacity Forms (RFC). You can get these from your attorney. The RFC form is not completed by you but by your doctor.

Did you find your Exertional level? Keep your finger on that Grid.

Age

AGE ALSO PLAYS AN IMPORTANT factor.

The older you are, the better chance you have of getting a disability.

If you are 18-49 years old, you are considered to be a "younger individual."

If you are 50-54 years old, you are considered to be "closely approaching advanced age."

If you are 55-59 years old, you are considered to be "advanced age."

If you are 60-64 years old, you are considered "closely approaching retirement age."

And, if you are 64-65 years old, you are considered "retirement age,"

Remember, the older you are, the easier it is to get approved for benefits. Find the column with your age and move your finger down that column.

Education

THE NEXT CATEGORY IS Education. Take your finger and find your education level.

Social Security has several categories of education. They range from Limited or Less (unable to read or write and/or did not obtain a high school diploma or pass a GED examination). The Next level is high school graduates or more.

Take your dinger and move it down the Education category until you reach the highest level of Education you have completed.

Skills

THE NEXT CATEGORY REQUIRES you to see if you have skills that you acquired from your past work and if they are transferable or non-transferable.

Continue using your finger to pick whether you have transferable skills or not. Again, this will usually be a determination made by the Judge based on the jobs you worked over the last 15 years.

Take your finger and continue down that column until you find it.

Did you find it?

Now look to the right and final column. The Grid will list out whether you are found "disabled" or "not disabled."

And that, my friends, are the instructions for reading the Grids.

It's not a perfect system, but it's the system of rules that Social Security currently has in place.

Determining your Grid Rule number should be part of your theory of the case in your opening statement to the Judge.

Grid Table When Maximum Sustained Work Capacity Limited to <u>Sedentary</u> Work

CAPABILITY TO SIT FOR up to 6 hours in an 8-hour day and lift up to 10 lbs. occasionally during a day

Rule	Age	Education	Previous Work	Decision
201.01	55+	Limited or less	Unskilled or none	**Disabled**
201.02	55+	Limited or less	Skilled or semi-skilled. Skills not transferrable	**Disabled**
201.03	55+	Limited or less	Skilled or semi-skilled. Skills transferrable	Not Disabled
201.04	55+	HS grad or more — does not provide for direct entry into skilled work	Unskilled or none	**Disabled**
201.05	55+	HS grad or more — provides for direct entry into skilled work	Unskilled or none	Not Disabled
201.06	55+	HS grad or more — does not provide for direct entry into skilled work	Skilled or semi-skilled; skills not transferrable	**Disabled**
201.07	55+	HS grad or more — does not provide for direct entry into skilled work	Skilled or semi-skilled; skills transferrable	Not Disabled
201.08	55+	HS grad or more — provides for direct entry into skilled work	Skilled or semi-skilled; skills not transferrable	Not Disabled
201.09	50-54	Limited or less	Unskilled or none	**Disabled**
201.10	50-54	Limited or less	Skilled or semi-skilled; skills not transferrable	**Disabled**
201.11	50-54	Limited or less	Skilled or semi-skilled; skills transferrable	Not Disabled
201.12	50-54	HS grad or more — does not provide for direct entry into skilled work	Unskilled or none	**Disabled**
201.13	50-54	HS grad or more — provides for direct entry into skilled work	Unskilled or none	Not Disabled
201.14	50-54	HS grad or more — does not provide for direct entry into skilled work	Skilled or semi-skilled; skills not transferrable	**Disabled**
201.15	50-54	HS grad or more — does not provide for direct entry into skilled work	Skilled or semi-skilled; skills transferrable	Not Disabled
201.16	50-54	HS grad or more — provides for direct entry into skilled work	Skilled or semi-skilled; skills not transferrable	Not Disabled
201.17	45-49	Illiterate or unable to communicate in English	Unskilled or none	**Disabled**

Rule	Age	Education	Previous Work	Decision
201.18	45-49	Limited or less but literate and able to communicate in English	Unskilled or none	Not Disabled
201.19	45-49	Limited or less	Skilled or semi-skilled; skills not transferrable	Not Disabled
201.20	45-49	Limited or less	Skilled or semi-skilled; skills transferrable	Not Disabled
201.21	45-49	HS grad or more	Skilled or semi-skilled; skills not transferrable	Not Disabled
201.22	45-49	HS grad or more	Skilled or semi-skilled; skills transferrable	Not Disabled

Grid Table When Maximum Sustained Work Capacity Limited to <u>Light</u> Work

CAPABILITY TO STAND and walk for up to 6 hours in an 8-hour day, lift 10 lbs. frequently and 20 lbs. occasionally

Rule	Age	Education	Previous Work	Decision
202.01	55+	Limited or less	Unskilled or none	**Disabled**
202.02	55+	Limited or less	Skilled or semi-skilled Skills not transferrable	**Disabled**
202.03	55+	Limited or less	Skilled or semi-skilled Skills transferrable	Not Disabled
202.04	55+	HS grad or more — does not provide for direct entry into skilled work	Unskilled or none	**Disabled**
202.05	55+	HS grad or more — provides for direct entry into skilled work	Unskilled or none	Not Disabled
202.06	55+	HS grad or more — does not provide for direct entry into skilled work	Skilled or semi-skilled Skills not transferrable	**Disabled**
202.07	55+	HS grad or more — does not provide for direct entry into skilled work	Skilled or semi-skilled Skills transferrable	Not Disabled
202.08	55+	HS grad or more — provides for direct entry into skilled work	Skilled or semi-skilled Skills not transferrable	Not Disabled
202.09	50-54	Illiterate or unable to communicate in English	Unskilled or none	**Disabled**
202.10	50-54	Limited or less — at least literate and able to communicate in English	Unskilled or none	Not Disabled
202.11	50-54	Limited or less	Skilled or semi-	Not Disable

Rule	Age	Education	Previous Work	Decision
			skilled Skills not transferrable	
202.12	50-54	Limited or less	Skilled or semi-skilled Skills transferrable	Not Disabled
202.13	50-54	HS grad or more	Unskilled or none	Not Disabled
202.14	50-54	HS grad or more	Skilled or semi-skilled Skills not transferrable	Not Disabled
202.15	50-54	HS grad or more	Skilled or semi-skilled Skills transferrable	Not Disabled

---

Grid Table When Maximum Sustained Work Capacity Limited to <u>Medium</u> Work

CAPABILITY TO STAND and walk for up to 6 hours in an 8-hour day, lift 50 lbs. frequently and 25 lbs. occasionally

Rule	Age	Education	Previous Work	De
203.01	60-64	Marginal or none	Unskilled or none	Di
203.02	60-64	Limited or less	None	Di
203.03	60-64	Limited	Unskilled	No Di
203.04	60-64	Limited or less	Skilled or semi-skilled Skills not transferrable	No Di
203.05	60-64	Limited or less	Skilled or semi-skilled Skills transferrable	No Di
203.06	60-64	HS grad or more	None or unskilled	No Di
203.07	60-64	HS grad or more — does not provide	Skilled or semi-skilled Skills not transferrable	No Di

Rule	Age	Education	Previous Work
		for direct entry into skilled work	
203.08	60-64	HS grad or more — does not provide for direct entry into skilled work	Skilled or semi-skilled Skills transferrable
203.09	60-64	HS grad or more — does provide for direct entry into skilled work	Skilled or semi-skilled Skills not transferrable
203.10	55+	Limited or less	None
203.11	55+	Limited or less	Unskilled

Rule	Age	Education	Previous Work	De
203.12	55+	Limited or less	Skilled or semi-skilled Skills not transferrable	No Dis
203.13	55+	Limited or less	Skilled or semi-skilled Skills transferrable	No Dis
203.14	55+	HS grad or more	None or unskilled	No Dis
203.15	55+	HS grad or more — does not provide for direct entry into skilled work	Skilled or semi-skilled Skills not transferrable	No Dis

Appendix C

Things to Think About

HERE ARE SOME THINGS to think about when considering if you should apply for benefits.

Of course, there are more medical conditions (unfortunately, the list never ends), but here are the most common medical conditions that my office encounters:

1. **Amputations**
   a. *When was your limb amputated?*
   b. *Do you use a prosthetic?*
   c. *Any difficulties?*

1. **Arthritis**
   a. *Where?*
   b. *Swelling?*
   c. *How long has it lasted?*
   d. *Need to elevate legs?*
   e. *How high?*
   f. *Swelling?*
   g. *Hands?*
   h. *Can you do buttons/zippers?*
   i. *Can openers?*
   j. *Type? Hold pencil?*
   k. *Drop things?*

1. **Asthma**
   a. *How often do you get attacks?*
   b. *Hospitalizations?*
   c. *Triggers for attacks?*
   d. *Breathing tests?*
   e. *Nebulizer? How many times a day?*

1. Cancer
    a. *What type?*
    b. *When did it start?*
    c. *Are you currently receiving treatments? Have you received treatment?*
    d. *What is the current status of your cancer?*
    e. *Weight loss?*
    f. *Hospitalizations?*

1. COPD
    a. *When did it start?*
    b. *Smoker?*
    c. *Breathing tests?*

1. Covid-19
    a. *When did you have Covid-19 last?*
    b. *Hospitalized?*
    c. *How long did you have COVID?*
    d. *Need for Oxygen?*
    e. *Since when?*
    f. *Do you know your oxygen levels?*

1. Dermatology/Skin Disorders
    a. *Describe the severity and current status of your impairment.*

1. Diabetes
    a. *Do you know your A1C?*
    b. *Is your diabetes controlled?*
    c. *Do you know your blood sugar in the morning?*
    d. *Do you have neuropathy?*
    e. *In your hands or feet or both?*
    f. *Need to elevate feet? How many hours a day?*
    g. *Diabetic ulcers?*
    h. *Vision problems?*

      i. *Need for naps?*

1. **Digestive System Issues/ Irritable Bowel Disorder**
   a. *Irritable bowel syndrome?*
   b. *How many times a day in the bathroom? How long do you spend in the bathroom each time you go?*
   c. *Accidents?*

1. **Eyes/Blind/Vision**
   a. *What is your prescription?*
   b. *Blind?*
   c. *Can you read a computer screen? Watch tv?*
   d. *If I toss a tennis ball at you, would you see it coming?*
   e. *Peripheral vision?*

1. **Fibromyalgia**
   a. *Have you had a Trigger point analysis?*
   b. *Rate 1-10*

1. **Headaches**
   a. *What is the frequency, and how long does a headache usually last?*
   b. *Rate 1-10*
   c. *Migraine auras? (floaters, stars, squiggly lines?)*

1. **Heart/Cardiac**
   a. *Do you know your ejection fraction?*
   b. *Any Heart attacks?*
   c. *When?*
   d. *How many?*
   e. *Any Hospitalizations?*
   f. *A-Fib?*
   g. *Stents?*
   h. *Transplants?*

1. Lupus
    a. *Fatigue?*
    b. *Weight loss? How much? Over a period of time?*
    c. *Difficulty walking?*
    d. *Assistive devices?*
    e. *How are your fine motor skills in your hands?*
    f. *Inflammation? Where?*
    g. *Can you perform Activities of Daily Living?*

1. Obesity
    a. *Weight and Height?*
    b. *Difficulty performing Activities of Daily Living?*

1. HIV
    a. *Do you know your T-cell count?*
    b. *Stomach problems?*
    c. *Loss of weight? Over how much time?*

1. Huntington's Disease
    a. *Since when?*
    b. *Ability to communicate?*
    c. *Walking? Standing? Sitting? Lifting?*
    d. *Assistive Device?*
    e. *Memory and Concentration?*

1. Kidney
    a. *Transplant?*
    b. *Are you receiving Dialysis?*
    c. *Since when?*
    d. *For how long will it continue?*

1. Liver
    a. *Describe the severity and current status of your impairment*

1. Mental Health

    a. **ADHD**

        i. *SSA does not consider this a disabling condition –*
        just part of the overall list of problems.

a. **Anxiety**

    i. *Do you have anxiety attacks? How often?*

    ii. *How do you interact with people?*

    iii. *Memory and concentration?*

    iv. *How often do you leave the house?*

    v. *Are you seeing a therapist? How often?*

    vi. *Are you on medications?*

    vii. *Are any current drugs or alcohol on your medical records?*

a. **Autism**

    i. *Testing?*

    ii. *When?*

    iii. *Results?*

    iv. *Memory/Concentration?*

    v. *Can you manage yourself?*

    vi. *Can you follow directions?*

    vii. *Interact with others?*

a. **Bi-polar**

    i. *How often do you get mania?*

    ii. *High or low?*

    iii. *How long does it last?*

    iv. *Unusual habits?*

    v. *How do you interact with people?*

    vi. *How often do you leave the house?*

    vii. *Are you seeing a therapist? How often?*

    viii. *Are you on medications?*

    ix. *Are any current drugs or alcohol on your medical records?*

a. **Depression**

    i. *Do you get crying spells?*

      ii. *Thoughts of hurting yourself?*
     iii. *Stay in a room or house for prolonged periods of time? How long*
     iv. *How often do you shower/change your clothing?*
      v. *Are you seeing a therapist? How often?*
     vi. *How often do you leave the house?*
    vii. *Are you on medications?*
   viii. *Are any current drugs or alcohol on your medical records?*

---

a. **PTSD**
      i. *What was the trauma (briefly – no need for a long story)*
     ii. *How long ago did the trauma occur?*
    iii. *Nightmares?*
    iv. *Flashbacks?*
     v. *How often do you leave the house?*
    vi. *Are you seeing a therapist? How often?*
   vii. *Are you on medications?*
  viii. *Are any current drugs or alcohol on your medical records?*

a. Schizophrenia:
      i. *Hallucinations? Seeing things? What do you see?*
     ii. *How often do you see them?*
    iii. *Do you hear things? What do you hear?*
    iv. *How often do you hear them?*
     v. *How often do you leave the house?*
    vi. *Are you seeing a therapist? How often?*
   vii. *Are you on medications?*
  viii. *Any current drugs or alcohol on your medical records?*

1. Motor Vehicle Accident?
   a. *When?*
   b. *Circumstances?*
   c. *Medical Conditions?*

1. **Multiple Sclerosis**
   a. *How is your walking? Standing? Balancing?*
   b. *Assistive device?*
   c. *Therapy?*
   d. *Memory and concentration?*
   e. *Interaction with others?*

1. **Muscular Dystrophy**
   a. *When? How long ago?*
   b. *Ability to communicate?*
   c. *Therapy?*
   d. *Walking? Standing? Sitting? Lifting?*
   e. *Assistive Device?*
   f. *Memory and Concentration?*

1. **Musculoskeletal (Ankles, Knees, Hips, Spine)**
   a. *Have you had an MRI in the last 2 years?*
   b. *Any Surgeries?*
   c. *Assistive device prescribed?*
   d. *Physical Therapy? Shots?*
   e. *How long can you stand?*
   f. *How far can you walk?*
   g. *How long can you sit?*
   h. *Do you need to elevate your legs?*
   i. *How many minutes/hours a day do you need to elevate them?*

1. **Parkinsonian Syndrome**
   a. *Fatigue?*
   b. *Weight loss? How much? Over a period of time?*
   c. *Difficulty walking?*
   d. *Assistive devices?*
   e. *How are your fine motor skills in your hands?*
   f. *Inflammation? Where?*
   g. *Can you perform Activities of Daily Living?*

1. Rheumatoid Arthritis
    a. *Fatigue?*
    b. *Weight loss? How much? Over a period of time?*
    c. *Difficulty walking?*
    d. *Assistive devices?*
    e. *How are your fine motor skills in your hands?*
    f. *Inflammation? Where?*
    g. *Can you perform Activities of Daily Living?*

1. Seizures/ Epilepsy
    a. *What type of seizures?*
    b. *Grand Mal, Freq.____*
    c. *Petite Mal, Freq.___*

1. Sjogren's Syndrome
    a. *Fatigue?*
    b. *Weight loss? How much? Over a period of time?*
    c. *Difficulty walking?*
    d. *Assistive devices?*
    e. *How are your fine motor skills in your hands?*
    f. *Inflammation? Where?*
    g. *Can you perform Activities of Daily Living?*

1. Stroke
    a. *When? How long ago?*
    b. *Ability to communicate?*
    c. *What happened to you as a result of the stroke?*
    d. *Walking? Standing? Sitting? Lifting?*
    e. *Assistive Device?*
    f. *Memory and Concentration?*

1. Traumatic Brain Injury
    a. *How is your walking? Standing? Balancing?*
    b. *Assistive device?*
    c. *Memory and concentration?*

d. *Interaction with others?*

Appendix D

BELOW ARE 2 DIFFERENT Residual Functional Capacity (RFC) **Questionnaires:**

1. **Physical, and**
2. **Mental**

I have also included a cover letter for you to send to your medical provider.

Both of these forms are essential for winning your disability case!

There are many different versions of RFCs that can be used, and each attorney's office has its own style. These are the versions that I use and which I have found great success.

Obviously, the "Physical" version should be used with any medical provider who treats you for physical conditions, and the "Mental" version should be used with your mental health provider.

I hope that they will help you with your case!

PHYSICAL RESIDUAL FUNCTIONAL CAPACITY QUESTIONNAIRE

NAME:

SSN:

Dear Dr.

_________________________________:

I have applied for either Supplemental Security Income (SSI) and/or Social Security Disability Insurance (SSDI) benefits with the Social Security Administration (SSA).

Please find attached a **Residual Functional Capacity (RFC)** questionnaire.

The completion of this questionnaire is essential to the outcome of my case.

If you have any questions or concerns regarding this request for information, please feel free to contact me at the telephone numbers that you have for me on file.

Please return it as soon as possible so that I can submit it for consideration to the SSA.

Very truly yours,

Your NAME and SIGNATURE

NAME: _________________________________

SSN: _______________________________

MEDICAL ASSESSMENT OF ABILITY TO DO
WORK-RELATED ACTIVITIES

In addition to your treatment/examination records for this patient, please provide a statement of the patient's impairment - related physical limitation as of the date of last visit or date of current examination, whichever is applicable.

A. ___ The patient has no impairment-related physical limitation, **OR**

B.   In relation to the impairment(s), the patient has the following exertional limitations. (Please explain any limitations.)

   1 <u>Occasionally</u> lift and/or carry (including upward pulling) for a total, of from very little up to 1/3 of an eight-hour workday (cumulative, not continuous) a maximum of:

     ___ less than 10 pounds   ___ 10 pounds

     ___ 20 pounds   ___ 50 pounds

     ___ 100 pounds   ___ cannot assess

     What are the medical findings that support this opinion?

   2. <u>Frequently</u> lift and/or carry for a total of from 1/3 to 2/3 of an eight-hour workday a maximum of:

     ___ less than 10 pounds   ___ 10 pounds

     ___ 20 pounds   ___ 50 pounds

     ___ 100 pounds   ___ cannot assess

     What are the medical findings that support this opinion?

3. Stand and/or walk (with normal breaks) for a total in an eight-hour workday:

    ___ less than two hours   ___ about two hours

    ___ about four hours   ___ six or more hours

    ___ cannot assess

        What are the medical findings that support this opinion?

____

4. Sit (with normal breaks) for a total in an eight-hour workday:

    ___ less than six hours   ___ about six hours

    ___ must periodically alternate sitting and standing to relieve pain or discomfort

    ___ cannot assess

        What are the medical findings that support this opinion?

____

5. Push and/or pull (including operation of hand and/or foot controls):

    ___ unlimitedly, other than as shown for lift and/or carry

    ___ limited in <u>upper</u> extremities (describe nature and degree)

    ___ limited in <u>lower</u> extremities (describe nature and degree)

    ___ cannot assess

        What are the medical findings that support this opinion?

____

6. Is there a documented medical need for a **walker**, **canes**, **crutches,** or other **assistive Devices**?

YES _________ NO _________

1. Use of the hands for fine and gross motor activities (including handling, fingering, and feeling):

__ less than occasionally (less than 1/3 of an 8-hour workday)

__ occasionally (at least 1/3 of an 8-hour workday)

__ frequently (up to 2/3 of an 8-hour workday)

__ constantly (the entire 8-hour workday)

1. Reaching in all directions:

__ less than occasionally (less than 1/3 of an 8-hour workday)

__ occasionally (at least 1/3 of an 8-hour workday)

__ frequently (up to 2/3 of an 8-hour workday)

__ constantly (the entire 8-hour workday)

1. Other significant limitations (postural, visual, communicative, or environmental): _______________________________

1. How many absences from work can be expected to occur per month?

_____0 _____1-2 _____3 plus

1. What percentage of the workday will the patient be "off task" due to physical impairments?

_____0 _____Less than 10% _____10-15% _____More than 15%

The foregoing restrictions have been present since:

____

______________ _________________ _______

Physician Name Physician Signature Date

MENTAL RESIDUAL FUNCTIONAL CAPACITY

QUESTIONNAIRE

NAME: _______________________________

SSN: _______________________________

Dear Dr.

_______________________________:I have applied for either Supplemental Security Income (SSI) and/or Social Security Disability Insurance (SSDI) benefits with the Social Security Administration (SSA).

Please find attached a **Residual Functional Capacity (RFC)** questionnaire.

The completion of this questionnaire is essential to the outcome of my case. If you have any questions or concerns regarding this request for information, please feel free to contact me at the telephone numbers that you have for me on file.

Please return it as soon as possible so that I can submit it for consideration to the SSA.

Very truly yours,

Your NAME and SIGNATURE

INSTRUCTIONS:

Please assist us in determining this individual's ability to do work-related activities on a sustained basis. "Sustained basis" means the ability to perform work-related activities eight hours a day for five days a week, or an equivalent work schedule. (SSR 96-8p). Please give us your professional opinion of <u>what the individual can still do despite his/her impairment(s)</u>. The opinion should be based on your findings with respect to medical history, clinical and laboratory findings, diagnosis, prescribed treatment and response, and prognosis.

For each activity shown below, respond to the questions about the individual's ability to perform the activity. When doing so, use the following definitions for the rating terms:

- None - Absent or minimal limitations. If limitations are present they are transient and/or expected reactions to psychological stresses.
- Mild - There is a slight limitation in this area, but the individual can generally function well.
- Moderate - There is more than a slight limitation in this area but the individual is still able to function satisfactorily.
- Marked - There is serious limitation in this area. There is a substantial loss in the ability to effectively function.
- Extreme - There is major limitation in this area. There is no useful ability to function in this area.

IT IS VERY IMPORTANT TO DESCRIBE THE FACTORS THAT SUPPORT YOUR ASSESSMENT. WE ARE REQUIRED TO CONSIDER THE EXTENT TO WHICH YOUR ASSESSMENT IS SUPPORTED.

(1) Is ability to understand, remember, and carry out instructions affected by the impairment? ☐ No ☐ Yes
If "no," go to question #2. If "yes," please check the appropriate block to describe the individual's restriction for the following work-related mental activities.

	None	Mild	Moderate	Marked	Extreme
Understand and remember simple instructions.	☐	☐	☐	☐	☐
Carry out simple instructions.	☐	☐	☐	☐	☐
The ability to make judgments on simple work-related decisions.	☐	☐	☐	☐	☐
Understand and remember complex instructions.	☐	☐	☐	☐	☐
Carry out complex instructions.	☐	☐	☐	☐	☐
The ability to make judgments on complex work-related decisions.	☐	☐	☐	☐	☐

Identify the factors (e.g., the particular medical signs, laboratory findings, or other factors described above) that support your assessment.

(2) Is ability to interact appropriately with supervision, co-workers, and the public, as well as respond to changes in the routine work setting, affected by impairments? ☐ No ☐ Yes
If "no," go to question #3. If "yes," please check the appropriate block to describe the individual's restriction for the following work-related mental activities.

	None	Mild	Moderate	Marked	Extreme
Interact appropriately with the public.	☐	☐	☐	☐	☐
Interact appropriately with supervisor(s).	☐	☐	☐	☐	☐
Interact appropriately with co-workers.	☐	☐	☐	☐	☐
Respond appropriately to usual work situations and to changes in a routine work setting.	☐	☐	☐	☐	☐

Identify the factors (e.g., the particular medical signs, laboratory findings, or other factors described above) that support your assessment.

(3) Are any other capabilities affected by the impairment? ☐ No ☐ Yes
If "yes," please identify the capability and describe how it is affected.

Identify the factors (e.g., the particular medical signs, laboratory findings, or other factors described above) that support your assessment.

(4) The limitations above are assumed to be your opinion regarding current limitations only.

However, if you have sufficient information to form an opinion within a reasonable degree of medical or psychological probability as to past limitations, on what date were the limitations you found above first present?_______

(5) If the claimant's impairment(s) include alcohol and/or substance abuse, do these impairments contribute to any of the claimant's limitations as set forth above? If so, please identify and explain what changes you would make to your answers if the claimant was totally abstinent from alcohol and/or substance use/abuse.

(6) HOW MANY ABSENCES from work can be expected to occur per month?

_____0 _____1-2 _____3 plus

(7) What percentage of the workday will the patient be "off task" due to psychological impairments?

_____0 _____Less than 10% _____10-15% ______More than 15%

(8) Can the individual manage benefits in his/her own best interest?

_____Yes _____No

(9) The foregoing restrictions have been present since:

____

______________ _________________ _________

Physician Name Physician Signature Date